WILLIAMS-SONOMA

MUFFINS

RECIPES AND TEXT
BETH HENSPERGER

GENERAL EDITOR
CHUCK WILLIAMS

PHOTOGRAPHS
NOEL BARNHURST

SIMON & SCHUSTER • SOURCE

NEW YORK • LONDON • TORONTO • SYDNEY • SINGAPORE

CONTENTS

THE CLASSICS

FRUIT MUFFINS

VEGETABLE MUFFINS

SAVORY MUFFINS

COFFEE CAKES

QUICK LOAF BREADS

INTRODUCTION

Of the many pleasures of home cooking, baking is high on my list. What makes the kitchen-tested recipes in this book especially enjoyable to prepare is that they are all easy to make. You do not have to knead dough or set it aside to rise. Instead, often within just an hour, your kitchen will be filled with the alluring aroma of freshly baked goods, followed by the appearance of muffins or perhaps a coffee cake or quick bread on your table. This ease of preparation is rewarding for all cooks, particularly if you are new to baking.

Regardless of your level of experience, you will appreciate the features in this book that enhance your knowledge of baking. Each recipe is accompanied by an illustrated side note about an essential ingredient or relevant technique. Before you make a recipe, you will want to read the detailed discussion at the back of the book covering such basics as mixing methods and baking pans. Whether you are new to baking or have spent many years in the kitchen, I am sure you will find recipes in these pages that will become a permanent part of your repertoire.

THE CLASSICS

The enticing aroma of muffins baking in a warm kitchen is an experience that everyone enjoys. Even more pleasurable are the results—tender, cakelike morsels that are so easy to make they have become a favorite of home bakers. Classic muffins such as blueberry, bran, and banana never cease to please, whether gracing the breakfast table or offered as an afternoon snack.

BLUEBERRY MUFFINS
10

HONEY-RAISIN BRAN MUFFINS
13

BANANA-WALNUT MUFFINS
14

LEMON-POPPY SEED MUFFINS
17

CRANBERRY-ORANGE MUFFINS
18

CINNAMON-BUTTERMILK MUFFINS
21

CHOCOLATE CHIP MUFFINS
22

BLUEBERRY MUFFINS

BLUEBERRIES

Plump blueberries, available from late spring through summer, are usually sold in pint boxes containing about 2 cups (8 oz/250 g) berries. The commercial berry is the North American high-bush variety, growing up to 15 feet high, primarily in Oregon, Washington, and Florida. Small, intensely flavored wild blueberries, native to New England and parts of Canada, can be used in this recipe as well. You can refrigerate berries for up to 2 days before using them. Do not wash them before storing, as the water will promote mold.

Preheat the oven to 375°F (190°C). Grease 12 standard muffin cups with butter or butter-flavored nonstick cooking spray.

To make the topping, stir together the flour, granulated sugar, brown sugar, and cinnamon in a small bowl. Using a pastry cutter or your fingers, cut or rub the butter into the dry ingredients just until coarse crumbs form. Alternatively, combine the dry ingredients and the butter in a food processor and pulse just until coarse crumbs form.

To make the muffins, in a bowl, using an electric mixer on medium speed, cream together the butter and sugar until light and fluffy. Add the eggs, one at a time, beating well after each addition until blended into the butter mixture.

In another bowl, stir together the flour, baking powder, and salt. Add the dry ingredients to the butter mixture in 2 increments, alternating with the milk and vanilla. Stir just until evenly moistened. The batter will be slightly lumpy. Using a large rubber spatula, gently fold in the blueberries just until evenly distributed, no more than a few strokes. Take care not to break up the fruit. Do not overmix.

Spoon the batter into each muffin cup, filling it level with the rim of the cup. Sprinkle each muffin with some topping.

Bake until golden, dry, and springy to the touch, 20–25 minutes. A toothpick inserted into the center of a muffin should come out clean. Transfer the pan to a wire rack and let cool for 5 minutes. Unmold the muffins. Serve warm or at room temperature, with maple butter.

MAKES 12 MUFFINS

FOR THE TOPPING:

¼ cup (1½ oz/45 g) all-purpose (plain) flour

2 tablespoons *each* granulated sugar and firmly packed light brown sugar

¼ teaspoon ground cinnamon

2 tablespoons cold unsalted butter, cut into small pieces

FOR THE MUFFINS:

7 tablespoons (3½ oz/ 105 g) unsalted butter, at room temperature

¾ cup (6 oz/185 g) granulated sugar

2 large eggs

2¼ cups (11½ oz/360 g) all-purpose (plain) flour

4 teaspoons baking powder

½ teaspoon salt

1 cup (8 fl oz/250 ml) milk

1½ teaspoons vanilla extract (essence)

1½ cups (6 oz/185 g) fresh blueberries or frozen unsweetened blueberries, unthawed

Maple Butter (page 107) for serving

HONEY-RAISIN BRAN MUFFINS

2 cups (10 oz/315 g) all-purpose (plain) flour

2 cups (8 oz/250 g) unprocessed bran flakes

1½ cups (9 oz/280 g) mixed dark and golden (sultana) raisins

⅓ cup (1 oz/30 g) toasted wheat germ

2 teaspoons baking soda (bicarbonate of soda)

1 teaspoon baking powder

1 teaspoon salt

½ cup (4 oz/125 g) unsalted butter, at room temperature

½ cup (3½ oz/105 g) firmly packed light or dark brown sugar

½ cup (6 oz/185 g) honey

1 cup (8 oz/250 g) plain yogurt

½ cup (4 fl oz/125 ml) buttermilk

2 teaspoons vanilla extract (essence)

3 large eggs, beaten

Preheat the oven to 400°F (200°C). Grease 18 standard muffin cups with butter or butter-flavored nonstick cooking spray; fill the unused cups one-third full with water to prevent warping.

In a bowl, stir together the flour, bran, raisins, wheat germ, baking soda, baking powder, and salt.

In another bowl, using a wooden spoon, cream together the butter, brown sugar, and honey until fluffy. Beat in the yogurt, then the buttermilk and vanilla, until well blended and smooth.

Make a well in the center of the dry ingredients and add the creamed mixture and the eggs. Beat just until evenly moistened. The batter will be thick and slightly lumpy. Do not overmix.

Spoon the batter into each muffin cup, filling it level with the rim of the cup.

Transfer the filled pan(s) to the oven and immediately reduce the oven temperature to 350°F (180°C). Bake until golden, dry, and springy to the touch, 18–22 minutes. A toothpick inserted into the center of a muffin should come out clean. Transfer the pan(s) to wire racks and let cool for at least 15 minutes. Unmold the muffins. Serve warm or at room temperature, with butter.

MAKES 18 MUFFINS

BRAN

Wheat bran, the outer layer of grains of wheat, is a by-product of the flour-milling process. Although almost tasteless, fresh bran con-tributes a mild earthy flavor to muffins and other baked goods and is added to recipes along with flour to boost the fiber content and overall nutrition. Unprocessed wheat bran, which has not been toasted, is also packaged as miller's bran. Look for it in the cereal section of super-markets or in natural-foods stores. Because bran is high in natural oils, it should be stored in the refrigerator to maintain freshness.

BANANA-WALNUT MUFFINS

Preheat the oven to 375°F (190°C). Grease 10 standard muffin cups with butter or butter-flavored nonstick cooking spray; fill the unused cups one-third full with water to prevent warping.

In a bowl, stir together the flour, sugar, chopped walnuts, baking soda, and salt.

In another bowl, whisk together the oil, egg, mashed bananas, and buttermilk until blended. Add the dry ingredients and beat well until evenly combined and creamy.

Spoon the batter into each muffin cup, filling it level with the rim of the cup.

Bake until golden, dry, and springy to the touch, 20–25 minutes. A toothpick inserted into the center of a muffin should come out clean. Transfer the pan to a wire rack and let cool for 5 minutes. Unmold the muffins. Serve them warm or at room temperature, with butter.

MAKES 10 MUFFINS

WALNUT OIL

Excellent for baking, walnut oil was once a specialty item but is now commonly sold in well-stocked supermarkets. The subtly flavored oil is extracted from raw walnut meats and is very nutritious and high in unsaturated fat. For this recipe, do not use toasted walnut oil, a favorite in French cooking, as it is not the same as plain walnut oil. To prevent the oil from becoming rancid, store it in the refrigerator. It will keep for up to 3 months. If you cannot find walnut oil, you may substitute canola oil in this muffin recipe.

1½ cups (7½ oz/235 g) all-purpose (plain) flour

¾ cup (6 oz/185 g) sugar

¾ cup (3 oz/90 g) walnuts, coarsely chopped

1½ teaspoons baking soda (bicarbonate of soda)

¼ teaspoon salt

½ cup (4 fl oz/125 ml) walnut oil or canola oil

1 large egg

2 or 3 medium to large very ripe bananas, slightly mashed to yield 1¼ cups (10 oz/315 g)

3 tablespoons buttermilk

LEMON-POPPY SEED MUFFINS

½ cup (4 oz/125 g) unsalted butter, at room temperature

⅔ cup (5 oz/155 g) lemon sugar *(far right)* or granulated sugar

2 large eggs, separated

1⅓ cups (7 oz/220 g) all-purpose (plain) flour

1 teaspoon baking powder

½ teaspoon baking soda (bicarbonate of soda)

2 tablespoons poppy seeds

Grated zest of 2 lemons

¼ teaspoon salt

½ cup (4 fl oz/125 ml) buttermilk

2 tablespoons strained fresh lemon juice

1 teaspoon vanilla extract (essence)

3 tablespoons coarse raw sugar for sprinkling

Lemon Curd (page 107) for serving

Preheat the oven to 350°F (180°C). Grease 10 standard muffin cups with butter or butter-flavored nonstick cooking spray or line with paper liners; fill the unused cups one-third full with water to prevent warping.

In a bowl, using an electric mixer on medium speed, cream the butter and sugar until light and fluffy. Add the egg yolks, one at a time, beating well after each addition until blended.

In another bowl, stir together the flour, baking powder, baking soda, poppy seeds, lemon zest, and salt. Using the mixer on low speed, add the dry ingredients to the creamed mixture in 2 increments, alternating with the buttermilk, then the lemon juice and vanilla. Beat just until smooth.

In a large bowl, using the mixer with spotlessly clean beaters on high speed or a balloon whisk, beat the egg whites just until they form soft peaks. Using a large rubber spatula, gently fold the egg whites into the batter until blended.

Spoon the batter into each muffin cup, filling it three-fourths full. Sprinkle the top of each muffin with some of the raw sugar.

Bake until golden, dry, and springy to the touch, 20–25 minutes. A toothpick inserted into the center of a muffin should come out clean. Transfer the pan to a wire rack and let cool for 5 minutes. Unmold the muffins and let cool completely. Serve them at room temperature, with lemon curd.

MAKES 10 MUFFINS

LEMON SUGAR

This simple recipe may be used to add lemon flavor to any recipe calling for sugar and lemon zest. Using a small paring knife or a vegetable peeler, remove the zest from 3 large lemons, leaving the bitter white pith behind; reserve the fruit and juice for another use. Place the zest in a food processor and add ½ cup (4 oz/120 g) granulated sugar. Pulse until the zest is evenly distributed. Add another ½ cup sugar and pulse until the zest is finely ground. Store in an airtight container in the refrigerator for up to 2 months. Makes about 1 cup (8 oz/250 g).

CRANBERRY-ORANGE MUFFINS

Preheat the oven to 375°F (190°C). Grease 10 standard muffin cups with butter or butter-flavored nonstick cooking spray; fill the unused cups one-third full with water to prevent warping.

In a bowl, stir together the flour, granulated sugar, brown sugar, baking powder, salt, and zest.

In another bowl, whisk together the egg, melted butter, milk, and orange juice until blended. Add to the dry ingredients, stirring just until evenly moistened. The batter will be slightly lumpy. Using a large rubber spatula, fold in the cranberries and nuts just until evenly distributed, no more than a few strokes. Do not overmix.

Spoon the batter into each muffin cup, filling it level with the rim of the cup.

Bake until golden, dry, and springy to the touch, 20–25 minutes. A toothpick inserted into the center of a muffin should come out clean. Transfer the pan to a wire rack and let cool for 5 minutes. Unmold the muffins. Serve them warm or at room temperature, with butter.

MAKES 10 MUFFINS

CRANBERRIES

Harvested from bogs when cold weather arrives and available throughout the winter months, tart, fresh cranberries are a signature fresh fruit of autumn and early winter. They are packaged in 12-ounce (375-g) plastic bags that contain 3 cups of berries. Cranberries can be enjoyed throughout the year by freezing them in airtight freezer bags; they keep for up to 1 year in perfect condition. The combination of tart cranberries sweetened with oranges, another fruit of winter, is one of the classic flavor pairings in baking.

2 cups (10 oz/315 g) all-purpose (plain) flour

½ cup (4 oz/125 g) granulated sugar

½ cup (3½ oz/105 g) firmly packed light brown sugar

2 teaspoons baking powder

½ teaspoon salt

Grated zest of 1 orange

1 large egg

4 tablespoons (2 oz/60 g) unsalted butter, melted, or walnut oil

½ cup (4 fl oz/125 ml) milk

½ cup (4 fl oz/125 ml) strained fresh orange juice

1½ cups (6 oz/185 g) fresh cranberries or frozen cranberries, unthawed

½ cup (2 oz/60 g) pecans or walnuts, chopped

CINNAMON-BUTTERMILK MUFFINS

FOR THE MUFFINS:

7 tablespoons (3½ oz/105 g) unsalted butter, at room temperature

⅔ cup (5 oz/155 g) sugar

1 large egg

1½ cups (7½ oz/235 g) all-purpose (plain) flour

1½ teaspoons baking powder

½ teaspoon baking soda (bicarbonate of soda)

½ teaspoon salt

½ teaspoon freshly grated nutmeg

½ cup (4 fl oz/125 ml) buttermilk

1½ teaspoons vanilla extract (essence)

FOR THE TOPPING:

⅔ cup (5 oz/155 g) sugar

1 tablespoon ground cinnamon

6 tablespoons (3 oz/90 g) unsalted butter, melted

Preheat the oven to 350°F (180°C). Grease 9 standard muffin cups with butter or butter-flavored nonstick cooking spray; fill the unused cups one-third full with water to prevent warping.

To make the muffins, in a bowl, using an electric mixer on medium speed, cream together the butter and sugar until light and fluffy. Add the egg, beating well until pale and smooth.

In another bowl, stir together the flour, baking powder, baking soda, salt, and nutmeg. Add to the butter mixture in 2 increments, alternating with the buttermilk and vanilla. Stir just until evenly moistened. The batter will be slightly lumpy.

Spoon the batter into each muffin cup, filling it three-fourths full. Bake until golden, dry, and springy to the touch, 20–25 minutes. A toothpick inserted into the center of a muffin should come out clean. Transfer the pan to a wire rack and let cool for 5 minutes. Unmold the muffins and let stand until cool enough to handle.

To make the topping, stir together the sugar and cinnamon in a small, shallow bowl. Have ready the melted butter in another small bowl. Holding the bottom of a muffin, dip the top into the melted butter, turning to coat it evenly. Immediately dip the top in the cinnamon-sugar mixture, coating it evenly, then tapping it to remove excess sugar. Transfer to the rack, right side up. Repeat with the remaining muffins. Let cool completely before serving.

Note: These cakelike muffins are made from a batter similar to that used for making donuts, but are baked instead of fried.

MAKES 9 MUFFINS

BUTTERMILK

Luscious buttermilk is a tangy, cultured milk product made by adding healthful bacteria to whole or low-fat milk. It has a slightly thick, creamlike consistency and gentle acidity that make it an excellent tenderizer in muffins and quick breads. Recipes using buttermilk usually call for baking soda, an alkaline leavener that reacts with the acidity in buttermilk. The resulting carbon dioxide bubbles expand in the heat of the oven, creating steam that helps produce rounded, moist muffins.

CHOCOLATE CHIP MUFFINS

SEMISWEET CHOCOLATE

Sweet and mellow semisweet chocolate is a combination of cocoa butter and chocolate liquor—the smooth brown paste that is ground from roasted cocoa beans—blended with sugar and vanilla for flavoring and with lecithin, a fatty plant-based additive that contributes a smooth texture. The chocolate is sold in bar form and as chips ranging in size from ½ inch (12 mm) to ⅛ inch (3 mm). In most recipes, including this one, semisweet chocolate can be used interchangeably with bittersweet chocolate, which is similar.

Preheat the oven to 350°F (180°C). Grease 12 standard muffin cups with butter or butter-flavored nonstick cooking spray or line with paper liners.

In a bowl, whisk together the melted butter, buttermilk, eggs, and vanilla until smooth.

In another bowl, stir together the flour, sugar, baking powder, baking soda, and salt. Make a well in the center and add the buttermilk mixture. Beat until smooth and well mixed, 1–2 minutes. Using a large rubber spatula, fold in the chocolate chips just until evenly distributed. Do not overmix.

Spoon the batter into each muffin cup, filling it level with the rim of the cup.

Bake until golden, dry, and springy to the touch, 20–25 minutes. A toothpick inserted into the center of a muffin should come out clean. Transfer the pan to a wire rack and let cool for 5 minutes. Unmold the muffins and let cool completely. Serve them at room temperature.

MAKES 12 MUFFINS

½ cup (4 oz/125 g) unsalted butter, melted

¾ cup (12 fl oz/375 ml) buttermilk

2 large eggs

1 tablespoon vanilla extract (essence)

2 cups (10 oz/315 g) all-purpose (plain) flour

¾ cup (6 oz/185 g) sugar

2 teaspoons baking powder

½ teaspoon baking soda (bicarbonate of soda)

½ teaspoon salt

2 cups (12 oz/375 g) semisweet (plain) chocolate chips

FRUIT MUFFINS

Fruits of the season are the perfect ingredients for muffins. Peaches, pears, berries, apples, and figs lend a natural sweetness to muffins, making them healthful alternatives to rich pastries and snacks. Serve any of these muffins for breakfast, or set them alongside fruit or vegetable salad for lunch or dinner, or offer them for dessert.

SOUR CHERRY MUFFINS
WITH COCONUT STREUSEL
26

COUNTRY APPLESAUCE MUFFINS
29

VANILLA-PEAR MUFFINS
30

JAM-FILLED MUFFINS
33

DRIED FIG MUFFINS
34

PEACH MELBA MUFFINS
37

BLACKBERRY MUFFINS
38

SOUR CHERRY MUFFINS WITH COCONUT STREUSEL

Preheat the oven to 375°F (190°C). Grease 12 standard muffin cups with butter or butter-flavored nonstick cooking spray.

To make the coconut streusel, stir together the brown sugar and flour in a small bowl. Using a pastry cutter or your fingers, cut or rub in the butter until the mixture is crumbly. Stir in the coconut. Set aside.

To make the muffins, in a bowl, stir together the flour, sugar, baking powder, and salt.

In another bowl, whisk together the melted butter, eggs, and half-and-half. Make a well in the center of the dry ingredients and add the egg mixture. Beat until thick and creamy. The batter will be slightly lumpy. Do not overmix.

Spoon the batter into each muffin cup, filling it one-third full. Drop in a few cherries, add batter just to cover, and then drop in a few more cherries. Spoon on more batter until the cups are filled level with the rims. Sprinkle each with 1 heaping tablespoon of coconut streusel.

Bake until golden, dry, and springy to the touch, 20–25 minutes. Transfer the pan to a wire rack and let cool for 5 minutes. Unmold the muffins. Serve warm or at room temperature.

MAKES 12 MUFFINS

SOUR CHERRIES

Smaller in size than sweet cherries and more elusive to find fresh, dark red sour cherries are too acidic to eat out of hand but are prized for baking. Also called tart cherries, they are a regional specialty grown in Michigan, the heart of cherry country. The main varieties are Early Richmond, Montmorency, and Morello. Sour cherries are available in jars and cans. Cherries packed in water, often labeled "pie cherries," retain a luscious tangy flavor that is excellent in muffins and scones.

FOR THE COCONUT STREUSEL:

⅓ cup (2½ oz/75 g) firmly packed light brown sugar

⅓ cup (2 oz/60 g) all-purpose (plain) flour

¼ cup (2 oz/60 g) cold unsalted butter, cut into small pieces

½ cup (1½ oz/45 g) sweetened flaked coconut

FOR THE MUFFINS:

2 cups (10 oz/315 g) all-purpose (plain) flour

½ cup (4 oz/125 g) granulated sugar

4 teaspoons baking powder

½ teaspoon salt

¼ cup (2 oz/60 g) unsalted butter, melted

2 large eggs, beaten

1 cup (8 fl oz/250 ml) half-and-half (half cream) or milk

16 oz (500 g) jarred or canned pitted sour red pie cherries, drained and dried on paper towels

COUNTRY APPLESAUCE MUFFINS

2 cups (10 oz/315 g)
all-purpose (plain) flour

1 cup (4 oz/125 g) walnuts,
coarsely chopped, or 1 cup
(6 oz/185 g) dark or golden
(sultana) raisins

⅔ cup (5 oz/155 g) sugar

2 teaspoons baking powder

½ teaspoon baking soda
(bicarbonate of soda)

½ teaspoon salt

1½ teaspoons ground
cinnamon

1 teaspoon ground allspice

⅓ cup (3 fl oz/80 ml)
almond oil, walnut oil, or
canola oil

1 large egg

1 heaping cup (9 oz/280 g)
applesauce (*far right;*
see Notes)

Preheat the oven to 350°F (180°C). Grease 12 standard muffin cups with butter or butter-flavored nonstick cooking spray.

In a bowl, stir together the flour, walnuts, sugar, baking powder, baking soda, salt, cinnamon, and allspice.

In another bowl, whisk together the oil, egg, and applesauce until smooth. Make a well in the center of the dry ingredients and stir in the applesauce mixture just until evenly moistened. The batter may seem dry at first, but it will loosen and smooth out as you beat the mixture.

Spoon the batter into each muffin cup, filling it level with the rim of the cup.

Bake until golden, dry, and springy to the touch, 25–30 minutes. A toothpick inserted into the center of a muffin should come out clean. Transfer the pan to a wire rack and let cool for 5 minutes. Unmold the muffins. Serve them warm or at room temperature, with butter.

Notes: When measuring the applesauce for this recipe, use a cup for measuring liquids, such as a glass measuring pitcher. This recipe may easily be doubled.

MAKES 12 MUFFINS

APPLESAUCE

Peel, core, and chop 2½ lb (1.25 kg) apples such as Granny Smith, Newtown pippin, or McIntosh. Place in a heavy saucepan with ⅓ cup (3 fl oz/ 80 ml) water. Bring to a boil, reduce the heat to a simmer, and cook, partially covered, stirring occasionally, until very soft, 20–30 minutes. Remove from the heat. Mash the apples with a fork or pass through a food mill. Taste and add sugar if needed. The applesauce can be stored for up to 2 weeks in the refrigerator. It can be used at room temperature or cold in this and other quick bread recipes. Makes about 2½ cups (22 oz/690 g).

VANILLA-PEAR MUFFINS

Preheat the oven to 350°F (180°C). Grease 14 standard muffin cups with butter or butter-flavored nonstick cooking spray; fill the unused cups one-third full with water to prevent warping.

To make the topping, stir together the sugar, walnuts, and cinnamon in a small bowl. Set aside.

To make the muffins, in a bowl, stir together the flour, sugar, cinnamon, nutmeg, baking powder, baking soda, and salt.

In another bowl, whisk together the eggs, oil, buttermilk, and vanilla until blended. Add the dry ingredients, stirring just until evenly moistened. The batter will be slightly lumpy. Using a large rubber spatula, gently fold in the pears and walnuts just until evenly distributed, no more than a few strokes. Take care not to break up the fruit. Do not overmix.

Spoon the batter into each muffin cup, filling it level with the rim. Sprinkle the muffins with the topping, dividing it evenly.

Bake until golden, dry, and springy to the touch, 20–25 minutes. A toothpick inserted into the center of a muffin should come out clean. Transfer the pan(s) to a wire rack and let cool for 5 minutes. Unmold the muffins. Serve them warm or at room temperature, with butter.

MAKES 14 MUFFINS

PEARS

The highest quality pear varieties found in the United States are grown in western states with temperate climates. For baking in muffins, select blemish-free pears that are slightly underripe and have their stems intact. They are ready when their flesh yields to gentle pressure at the stem end but is still firm enough to chop into pieces. Baking varieties include the bell-shaped, yellow or red Bartlett (also known as Williams), the light green Anjou, the long-necked, speckled Bosc, the small Seckel, and the juicy, plump Comice.

FOR THE TOPPING:

3 tablespoons sugar

2 tablespoons chopped walnuts, ground

¼ teaspoon ground cinnamon

FOR THE MUFFINS:

2 cups (10 oz/315 g) all-purpose (plain) flour

½ cup (4 oz/125 g) sugar

2 teaspoons ground cinnamon

1 teaspoon freshly grated nutmeg

2 teaspoons baking powder

½ teaspoon *each* baking soda (bicarbonate of soda) and salt

2 large eggs

½ cup (4 fl oz/125 ml) canola oil or walnut oil

¾ cup (6 fl oz/180 ml) buttermilk

2 teaspoons vanilla extract (essence)

4 or 5 firm, ripe pears, 2 lb (1 kg) total weight, peeled, cored, and coarsely chopped

1 cup (4 oz/125 g) walnuts, coarsely chopped

JAM-FILLED MUFFINS

2 cups (10 oz/315 g)
all-purpose (plain) flour

¾ cup (6 oz/185 g) sugar

1 tablespoon baking
powder

½ teaspoon baking soda
(bicarbonate of soda)

½ teaspoon salt

6 tablespoons (3 oz/90 g)
unsalted butter, melted

2 large eggs

1 teaspoon vanilla extract
(essence)

¼ teaspoon almond
extract (essence)

1¼ cups (10 oz/315 g)
sour cream

⅓–½ cup (4–5 oz/
125–155 g) jelly or seedless
jam, such as red currant
jelly or raspberry, blackberry, or strawberry jam

Preheat the oven to 375°F (190°C). Grease 12 standard muffin cups with butter or butter-flavored nonstick cooking spray.

In a bowl, stir together the flour, sugar, baking powder, baking soda, and salt.

In another bowl, whisk together the melted butter, eggs, vanilla and almond extracts, and sour cream until smooth. Add the egg mixture to the dry ingredients and stir just until evenly moistened. The batter will be slightly lumpy. Do not overmix.

Spoon the batter into each muffin cup, filling it one-third full. Drop a heaping teaspoonful of jelly or jam into the center, then cover with batter level with the rim of the cup.

Bake until golden, dry, and springy to the touch, 20–25 minutes. Transfer the pan to a wire rack and let cool for 5 minutes. Unmold the muffins. Serve warm or at room temperature.

MAKES 12 MUFFINS

JELLY AND JAM
Sweet, spreadable fruit preserves, whether purchased or homemade, are musts on the breakfast table, and baked inside these tender, rich, sour cream muffins, they offer a colorful and tasty surprise. Jelly and jam make equally delicious fillings. Jellies, such as red currant, have been strained to achieve a firm, crystalline, silken-smooth result. By contrast, raspberry, blackberry, and strawberry jams are made with whole berries and therefore have a chunky texture. Trying various jams or jellies will result in a different muffin with every batch.

DRIED FIG MUFFINS

In a small saucepan, heat the apple juice and butter over medium-low heat until the butter is melted, about 5 minutes. Remove from the heat and add the figs and orange zest. Set aside until the mixture is room temperature and the figs are softened, about 1 hour.

Preheat the oven to 375°F (190°C). Grease 11 standard muffin cups with butter or butter-flavored nonstick cooking spray or line with paper liners; fill the unused cup one-third full with water to prevent warping.

In a bowl, stir together the flour, granulated and brown sugars, baking powder, and salt. Make a well in the center and add the cooled fig mixture, eggs, and vanilla. Stir just until evenly moistened. The batter will be slightly lumpy. Do not overmix.

Spoon the batter into each muffin cup, filling it level with the rim of the cup.

Bake until golden, dry, and springy to the touch, 20–25 minutes. A toothpick inserted into the center of a muffin should come out clean. Transfer the pan to a wire rack and let cool for 5 minutes. Unmold the muffins and let cool completely. Serve them at room temperature.

MAKES 11 MUFFINS

DRIED FIGS

Sweet, chewy dried figs are among the fruits favored for use in baking recipes. Choose either the pale Calimyrna, the most common variety found dried, or the dark purple, Black Mission fig. Dried whole figs tend to be very stiff because the drying process needs to permeate the entire fruit; therefore, softening them first is important to the texture of the finished muffins. Here, the figs are macerated in hot apple juice so they turn a lovely mahogany color and give off an enticing perfume.

1 cup (8 fl oz/250 ml) apple juice

6 tablespoons (3 oz/90 g) unsalted butter, cut into small pieces

12 oz (375 g) dried figs, stemmed and quartered

Grated zest of 1 large orange

2 cups (10 oz/315 g) all-purpose (plain) flour

½ cup (4 oz/125 g) granulated sugar

¼ cup (2 oz/60 g) firmly packed dark brown sugar

2½ teaspoons baking powder

½ teaspoon salt

2 large eggs, beaten

1½ teaspoons vanilla extract (essence)

PEACH MELBA MUFFINS

1 cup (4 oz/125 g) fresh raspberries or frozen unsweetened raspberries, unthawed

½ cup (4 oz/125 g) sugar, plus 2 tablespoons

1 tablespoon berry liqueur, such as Chambord, or raspberry vinegar

2 cups (10 oz/315 g) all-purpose (plain) flour

2½ teaspoons baking powder

½ teaspoon salt

2 large eggs

6 tablespoons (3 oz/90 g) unsalted butter, melted

1 cup (8 fl oz/250 ml) milk

1 or 2 peaches, about 8 oz (250 g) each, peeled, pitted, and coarsely chopped

¼ cup (1 oz/30 g) sliced (flaked) almonds for sprinkling

Preheat the oven to 375°F (190°C). Grease 11 standard muffin cups with butter or butter-flavored nonstick cooking spray; fill the unused cup one-third full with water to prevent warping.

In a small bowl, toss the raspberries with 1 tablespoon of the sugar and the liqueur. Let stand for 30 minutes.

In a bowl, stir together the flour, ½ cup (4 oz/125 g) sugar, baking powder, and salt.

In another bowl, whisk together the eggs, melted butter, and milk until blended. Stir in the dry ingredients just until evenly moistened, no more than 15–20 strokes. The batter will be slightly lumpy. Using a large rubber spatula, gently fold in the peaches just until evenly distributed, no more than a few strokes. Take care not to break up the fruit. Do not overmix.

Spoon the batter into each muffin cup, filling it half full. Divide the raspberries among the cups, using about 1 tablespoon per muffin, then cover with batter level with the rim of the cup. Sprinkle with the remaining 1 tablespoon sugar and the sliced almonds, dividing evenly.

Bake until golden, dry, and springy to the touch, 25–30 minutes. Transfer the pan to a wire rack and let cool for 5 minutes. Unmold the muffins. Serve them warm or at room temperature, with butter.

MAKES 11 MUFFINS

PEACH MELBA

This muffin recipe is based on Peach Melba, a classic dessert with fresh poached peach halves filled with vanilla ice cream. Topping the ice cream is a raspberry sauce—called "Melba sauce"—and a sprinkling of toasted almonds. The dish is the gustatory handiwork of the legendary French chef Auguste Escoffier, who created the combination in the late 1800s to honor Dame Nellie Melba, the most popular opera star of the day, who ate in his restaurant. The combination of sweet peaches and tart raspberries is a delectable treat.

BLACKBERRY MUFFINS

Preheat the oven to 375°F (190°C). Grease 12 standard muffin cups with butter or butter-flavored nonstick cooking spray.

To make the topping, stir together the sugar, flour, and zest in a small bowl. Stir in the melted butter until the mixture is crumbly. Add the pecans and stir to combine. Set aside.

To make the muffins, in a bowl, stir together the flour, sugar, baking powder, baking soda, cinnamon, zest, and salt. Make a well in the center and add the egg, melted butter, and buttermilk. Stir just until evenly moistened. The batter will be slightly lumpy. Sprinkle with the blackberries and gently fold in with a large rubber spatula just until evenly distributed, no more than a few strokes. Take care not to break up the fruit. Do not overmix.

Spoon the batter into each muffin cup, filling it to a bit above the rim of the cup. Top each muffin with the topping, dividing it evenly (the sugar will melt and produce a glaze effect).

Bake until golden, dry, and springy to the touch, 25–30 minutes. A toothpick inserted into the center of a muffin should come out clean. Transfer the pan to a wire rack and let cool for 10 minutes. Unmold the muffins. Serve them warm or at room temperature, with butter.

MAKES 12 MUFFINS

HANDLING BERRIES

The abundance of fresh ripe berries is one of the pleasures of summer. Each variety in the seasonal trinity—blackberries, blueberries, and raspberries—works beautifully in this recipe.

Remember to treat fresh berries gently after purchase. If not using them immediately, store them for up to 2 days in the refrigerator. Rinse the berries briefly in a colander before use, then pick over the berries and discard any that are moldy or mushy. Let dry in the colander or on a layer of paper towels.

FOR THE TOPPING:

⅓ cup (3 oz/90 g) sugar

3 tablespoons all-purpose (plain) flour

Grated zest of ½ lemon

2 tablespoons unsalted butter, melted

⅓ cup (1½ oz/45 g) pecans, finely chopped

FOR THE MUFFINS:

2 cups (10 oz/315 g) all-purpose (plain) flour

¾ cup (6 oz/185 g) sugar

2 teaspoons baking powder

½ teaspoon baking soda (bicarbonate of soda)

½ teaspoon ground cinnamon

Grated zest of ½ lemon

¼ teaspoon salt

1 large egg, beaten

5 tablespoons (2½ oz/75 g) unsalted butter, melted

1 cup (8 fl oz/250 ml) buttermilk

2 cups (8 oz/250 g) fresh blackberries or 2½ cups (10 oz/315 g) frozen unsweetened blackberries, unthawed

VEGETABLE MUFFINS

Whether you grow your own or buy them at a farmers' or produce market, vegetables in season are an inspiration to the creative baker. Muffins made with tomatoes, zucchini, chiles, carrots, sweet potatoes, and corn boast freshness and flavor in every bite. Enjoy this bountiful harvest of easy-to-prepare muffins, some of them sweet, others savory.

CARROT-NUT MUFFINS

Preheat the oven to 350°F (180°C). Grease 24 standard muffin cups with butter or butter-flavored nonstick cooking spray.

In a large bowl, combine the eggs, oil, and sugar. Using a whisk or an electric mixer on medium speed, vigorously beat just until smooth and slightly thickened, 1 full minute.

In another bowl, stir together the flour, baking powder, baking soda, salt, cinnamon, and allspice. Add to the egg mixture and, using the mixer on low speed or a wooden spoon, beat until smooth. Using a large rubber spatula, fold in the carrots and nuts, about 20 strokes. Scrape down the sides of the bowl and stir again.

Spoon the batter into each muffin cup, filling it no more than three-fourths full.

Bake until golden, dry, and springy to the touch, 20–25 minutes. A toothpick inserted into the center of a muffin should come out clean. Transfer the pans to wire racks and let cool for 5 minutes. Unmold the muffins. Serve warm or at room temperature.

MAKES 24 MUFFINS

SHREDDING VS. GRATING

Shredding refers to the process of cutting food into thin, narrow strips. One of the easiest ways to do this is to use the largest holes of a box grater-shredder, which are ideal for shredding vegetables such as carrots as well as medium soft cheeses such as Cheddar. Grating, on the other hand, is the process of reducing foods, such as lemon zest or hard Parmesan cheese, into tiny particles using the finest rasps of a grater-shredder. You may also shred and grate foods using a mandoline or food processor fitted with the appropriate disk.

4 large eggs

1 cup (8 fl oz/250 ml) canola oil or walnut oil

2 cups (1 lb/500 g) sugar

3 cups (15 oz/470 g) all-purpose (plain) flour

2 teaspoons baking powder

1 teaspoon baking soda (bicarbonate of soda)

½ teaspoon salt

2 teaspoons ground cinnamon

¼ teaspoon ground allspice

3 or 4 carrots, 12 oz (375 g) total weight, peeled and shredded

1½ cups (6 oz/185 g) walnuts, pecans, or hazelnuts, coarsely chopped

ZUCCHINI MUFFINS

1½ cups (7½ oz/235 g) all-purpose (plain) flour

¾ cup (6 oz/185 g) sugar

2 teaspoons baking powder

¼ teaspoon baking soda (bicarbonate of soda)

¼ teaspoon salt

½ teaspoon ground cinnamon

2 large eggs

⅓ cup (3 fl oz/80 ml) canola oil or almond oil

¼ cup (2½ oz/75 g) orange marmalade

1 teaspoon vanilla extract (essence)

1 zucchini, 4 oz (125 g) total weight, shredded and drained on paper towels

¾ cup (3 oz/90 g) dark raisins or dried sweet cherries

¼ cup (1 oz/30 g) pecans or almonds, chopped

Preheat the oven to 400°F (200°C). Grease 10 standard muffin cups with butter or butter-flavored nonstick cooking spray; fill the unused cups one-third full with water to prevent warping.

In a bowl, stir together the flour, sugar, baking powder, baking soda, salt, and cinnamon.

In another bowl, whisk together the eggs, oil, marmalade, vanilla, and zucchini until blended. Add the dry ingredients to the zucchini mixture in 3 increments and beat just until evenly moistened and smooth. Stir in the raisins and nuts just until evenly distributed. The batter will be stiff.

Spoon the batter into each muffin cup, filling it no more than three-fourths full.

Bake until golden, dry, and springy to the touch, 17–20 minutes. A toothpick inserted into the center of a muffin should come out clean. Transfer the pan to a wire rack and let cool for 5 minutes. Unmold the muffins. Serve them warm or at room temperature, with butter.

MAKES 10 MUFFINS

ZUCCHINI

The long, straight-necked zucchini is by far the best known and most popular of the summer squashes. These dark green or bright gold squashes are actually gourds, just like winter squashes, but are harvested when they are immature and their seeds and skin are sweet and tender. Known as *courgette* in France and England, the zucchini is harvested from a plant that originated in Italian home gardens. Before using the zucchini in this recipe, rinse and dry, then cut off the stem end before shredding (page 42) onto layers of paper towels to absorb some of the excess moisture.

JALAPEÑO-CORNMEAL MUFFINS

Preheat the oven to 400°F (200°C). Grease 11 standard muffin cups with butter or butter-flavored nonstick cooking spray; fill the unused cup one-third full with water to prevent warping.

In a bowl, stir together the cornmeal, flour, sugar, baking powder, and salt. Stir in the jalapeño chiles and zucchini and toss to distribute evenly.

Make a well in the center of the dry ingredients and add the oil, eggs, and buttermilk. Stir just until evenly moistened, using no more than 15–20 strokes. The batter will be slightly lumpy.

Spoon the batter into each muffin cup, filling it level with the rim of the cup. Sprinkle each muffin with some of the cheese.

Bake until golden, dry, and springy to the touch, about 25 minutes. A toothpick inserted into the center of a muffin should come out clean. Remove from the oven and immediately unmold the muffins onto a wire rack. Serve them hot, warm, or at room temperature, with butter.

MAKES 11 MUFFINS

JALAPEÑO CHILES

The thumb-sized jalapeño chile has thick flesh that may be green or red and can range from mildly hot to fiery. When working with jalapeños or other hot chiles, it is advisable to wear rubber gloves to prevent burns. The heat from a chile, carried in the membranes, can linger for hours on your skin, so thoroughly wash your hands, and the cutting board and knife, with hot, soapy water as soon as you finish working. For mild-flavored muffins use 2 chiles; to add more heat, use 3 chiles.

1¼ cups (7½ oz/235 g) fine- or medium-grind yellow cornmeal, preferably stone-ground

1¼ cups (6½ oz/200 g) all-purpose (plain) flour

3 tablespoons sugar

2½ teaspoons baking powder

1 teaspoon salt

2 or 3 green jalapeño chiles, seeded and minced

1 zucchini (4 oz/125 g), shredded

¼ cup (2 fl oz/60 ml) olive oil or sesame oil

2 large eggs, beaten

1½ cups (12 fl oz/375 ml) buttermilk

3 tablespoons grated Parmesan or Asiago cheese for sprinkling

TOMATO AND GOAT CHEESE MUFFINS

6 tablespoons (3 oz/90 g) unsalted butter

4 small green (spring) onions, including 1 inch (2.5 cm) of the tender green parts, finely chopped

2½ tablespoons minced fresh basil

1½ cups (7½ oz/235 g) all-purpose (plain) flour

1 cup (4½ oz/140 g) garbanzo flour

3½ teaspoons baking powder

½ teaspoon salt

1¼ cups (10 fl oz/310 ml) milk

2 large eggs

3 oz (90 g) fresh white goat cheese, divided into 10 equal portions

2 plum (Roma) tomatoes, halved lengthwise, then each half cut into 3 chunks

Preheat the oven to 400°F (200°C). Grease 10 standard muffin cups with butter or butter-flavored nonstick cooking spray; fill the unused cups one-third full with water to prevent warping.

In a small frying pan over low heat, melt the butter. Add the green onions and sauté until almost translucent, 1–2 minutes. Stir in the basil. Remove from the heat and set aside.

In a bowl, stir together the all-purpose and garbanzo flours, baking powder, and salt.

In another bowl, whisk together the milk and eggs until blended. Make a well in the center of the dry ingredients, then pour in the milk mixture and the butter mixture. Stir just until evenly moistened, using no more than 15–20 strokes. The batter will be thick and lumpy.

Spoon the batter into each muffin cup, filling it half full. Shape each portion of goat cheese into a round and set it in the center of the muffin batter. Place 1 or 2 tomato chunks on top of the cheese and gently press into the batter. Cover the cheese and tomato with batter until level with the rim of the cup.

Bake until golden, dry, and springy to the touch, 18–22 minutes. Do not overbake. To check the muffins, carefully lift a muffin from the pan; the sides should be browned. Transfer the pan to a wire rack and let cool for 5 minutes. Unmold the muffins. Serve warm or at room temperature.

MAKES 10 MUFFINS

GARBANZO FLOUR

This flour, ground from dried chickpeas and therefore also known as chickpea flour, is a staple in the Mediterranean and Middle East, where it is used to make flatbreads, fritters, and savory pancakes. It is also an ingredient in the breads and pancakes made by Indian cooks. The flour has a distinctive and very appealing, naturally sweet flavor. It may be difficult to find on supermarket shelves. If this is the case, look for it in natural-foods stores or in Indian markets, where it is sometimes labeled *besan*.

ONION AND SHALLOT MUFFINS

Preheat the oven to 375°F (190°C). Grease 11 standard muffin cups with butter or butter-flavored nonstick cooking spray; fill the unused cup one-third full with water to prevent warping.

In a frying pan over medium heat, heat 3 tablespoons of the oil. Add the onion and shallot; sauté until translucent, 2–3 minutes. Remove from the heat and let cool.

In a bowl, stir together the flour, 1 cup (4 oz / 125 g) of the cheese, and the parsley, baking powder, salt, oregano, and celery seed.

In another bowl, whisk together the eggs, remaining 2 tablespoons oil, and milk until blended. Add the cooled onions, along with any oil left in the pan. Make a well in the center of the dry ingredients and stir in the onion mixture just until evenly moistened. The batter will be slightly lumpy.

Spoon the batter into each muffin cup, filling it level with the rim of the cup. Sprinkle each muffin with some of the remaining ⅓ cup (1½ oz / 45 g) cheese.

Bake until golden, dry, and springy to the touch, 25–30 minutes. A toothpick inserted into the center of a muffin should come out clean. Transfer the pan to a wire rack and let cool for 5 minutes. Unmold the muffins. Serve warm or at room temperature.

MAKES 11 MUFFINS

SHALLOTS

Because of their delicate shape and color, shallots have a reputation for elegance. This diminutive member of the onion family grows in clusters of cloves like garlic and has a papery reddish or bronze skin. The white flesh lightly streaked with purple has a subdued onion flavor and cooks more quickly than the flesh of larger onions. To prepare a shallot, cut off both ends, then peel off the papery skin. Cut the bulb in half lengthwise and mince.

5 tablespoons (3 fl oz / 80 ml) olive oil

¼ cup (1½ oz / 45 g) finely chopped red onion

1 medium to large shallot, minced

3 cups (15 oz / 470 g) all-purpose (plain) flour

1⅓ cups (5½ oz / 170 g) grated Jarlsberg or Swiss cheese

3 tablespoons minced fresh flat-leaf (Italian) parsley

4 teaspoons baking powder

1½ teaspoons salt

1 teaspoon crumbled dried oregano or marjoram

½ teaspoon celery seed

2 large eggs

1 cup (8 fl oz / 250 ml) milk

CINNAMON-CRUNCH SWEET POTATO MUFFINS

FOR THE TOPPING:

3 tablespoons sugar

1 teaspoon ground
cinnamon

FOR THE MUFFINS:

2 sweet potatoes or yams
(orange-fleshed sweet
potatoes), 14 oz (440 g)
total weight, peeled and
cut into chunks

1¾ cups (9 oz/280 g)
all-purpose (plain) flour

½ teaspoon ground
cinnamon

½ teaspoon freshly grated
nutmeg

2 teaspoons baking powder

½ teaspoon salt

2 large eggs

½ cup (4 oz/125 g) sugar

½ cup (4 fl oz/125 ml)
canola oil or walnut oil

½ cup (4 fl oz/125 ml) milk

½ teaspoon orange oil, or
grated zest of 1 orange

¾ cup (3 oz/90 g) pecans,
coarsely chopped

To make the topping, stir together the sugar and cinnamon in a small bowl. Set aside.

To make the muffins, bring a saucepan of water to a boil, add the sweet potatoes, and cook until tender, 15–20 minutes. Remove from the heat and drain thoroughly. Transfer to a food processor and pulse until slightly fluffy. Scrape into a bowl and let cool to room temperature.

Preheat the oven to 400°F (200°C). Grease 12 standard muffin cups with butter or butter-flavored nonstick cooking spray.

In a bowl, stir together the flour, cinnamon, nutmeg, baking powder, and salt.

In another bowl, combine the eggs, sugar, oil, milk, and orange oil. Whisk vigorously for 1 minute. Add the mashed sweet potatoes and beat until completely blended. Add the dry ingredients and stir just until evenly moistened. The batter will be slightly lumpy. Using a large rubber spatula, fold in the pecans just until evenly distributed, no more than a few strokes. Do not overmix.

Spoon the batter into each muffin cup, filling it three-fourths full. Sprinkle with the topping, dividing evenly.

Bake until golden, dry, and springy to the touch, 20–25 minutes. A toothpick inserted into the center of a muffin should come out clean. Transfer the pan to a wire rack and let cool for 5 minutes. Unmold the muffins. Serve warm, with butter.

Note: Canned sweet potatoes or yams may be substituted for fresh. Drain them well before mashing.

MAKES 12 MUFFINS

SWEET POTATOES

These plump edible roots are available year-round but are most abundant in markets in autumn and winter. Some of these vegetables—members of the morning glory family—have tan skin and light yellow flesh; others have darker red-orange skin and flesh. The latter type is often called a yam in the United States, although it is not a true yam. Red-orange sweet potatoes are slightly moister and sweeter than the tan variety, which has the same texture as a russet potato when cooked and mashed.

SAVORY MUFFINS

Muffins are customarily thought of as sweet treats, but they can also be savory little breads. Sporting cheeses, vegetables, bacon, herbs, and hearty grains, these muffins make satisfying partners to soups, salads, and stews. Some, such as Muffins Florentine and Bacon and Gruyère Muffins, are a meal in themselves.

WHOLE-WHEAT DINNER MUFFINS

WHOLE-WHEAT FLOUR
Known for its nutty, sweet flavor and aroma and its extra nutrition, whole-wheat flour is ground from the entire kernel of wheat. By contrast, all-purpose (plain) flour has had the bran and germ removed. Commercial whole-wheat flours vary from fine to more coarsely ground; the grinds may be used interchangeably in recipes. To produce fine grinds, all parts of the grain are equally ground. Medium and coarse grinds have varying amounts of bran dispersed throughout.

Preheat the oven to 375°F (190°C). Grease 9 standard muffin cups with butter or butter-flavored nonstick cooking spray; fill the unused cups one-third full with water to prevent warping.

In a bowl, stir together the flour, cornmeal, brown sugar, baking powder, baking soda, and salt.

In another bowl, whisk together the egg yolks, butter, buttermilk, sour cream, and vanilla until blended. Stir the buttermilk mixture into the dry ingredients just until evenly moistened. The batter will be slightly lumpy.

In a large bowl, using an electric mixer with spotlessly clean beaters on medium speed or a balloon whisk, beat the egg whites just until they form soft peaks. Using a large rubber spatula, gently fold the egg whites into the batter until blended.

Spoon the batter into each muffin cup, filling it level with the rim of the cup. Sprinkle each muffin with some of the sesame seeds.

Bake until golden, dry, and springy to the touch, 20–25 minutes. A toothpick inserted into the center of a muffin should come out clean. Transfer the pan to a wire rack and let cool for 5 minutes. Unmold the muffins. Serve them warm or at room temperature, with butter.

MAKES 9 MUFFINS

1¼ cups (6½ oz/200 g) whole-wheat or graham flour

2 tablespoons yellow cornmeal

3 tablespoons firmly packed light or dark brown sugar

2 teaspoons baking powder

½ teaspoon baking soda (bicarbonate of soda)

½ teaspoon salt

2 large eggs, separated

3 tablespoons unsalted butter, melted, or sesame oil or olive oil

1 cup (8 fl oz/250 ml) buttermilk

2 tablespoons sour cream or plain yogurt

1 teaspoon vanilla extract (essence)

1½ tablespoons sesame seeds for sprinkling

CHEDDAR CHEESE MUFFINS

1¾ cups (9 oz/280 g) all-purpose (plain) flour

1¼ cups (5 oz/155 g) shredded sharp Cheddar cheese

2 tablespoons sugar

1 tablespoon baking powder

½ teaspoon salt

¼ teaspoon chili powder

1 large egg

3 tablespoons olive oil

1 cup (8 fl oz/250 ml) milk

1 tablespoon sesame seeds or 1½ teaspoons poppy seeds for sprinkling

Preheat the oven to 375°F (190°C). Grease 7 standard muffin cups with butter or butter-flavored nonstick cooking spray; fill the unused cups one-third full with water to prevent warping.

In a bowl, stir together the flour, cheese, sugar, baking powder, salt, and chili powder.

In another bowl, whisk together the egg, olive oil, and milk until blended. Make a well in the center of the dry ingredients, add the milk mixture, and stir just until evenly moistened. The batter will be slightly lumpy.

Spoon the batter into each muffin cup, filling it level with the rim of the cup. Sprinkle each muffin with some of the sesame seeds.

Bake until golden, dry, and springy to the touch, 20–25 minutes. A toothpick inserted into the center of a muffin should come out clean. Transfer the pan to a wire rack and let cool for 5 minutes. Unmold the muffins. Serve them warm or at room temperature, with butter.

Serving Tip: Try serving these muffins with hot-pepper jelly. The jelly, usually made with jalapeño chiles in combination with sweet peppers, is available in well-stocked markets and specialty-food stores.

MAKES 7 MUFFINS

SESAME SEEDS

Used as a garnish, tiny, flat sesame seeds contribute a subtle nutty flavor and crunchy texture to baked goods such as muffins and breads and to many other dishes both savory and sweet. The seeds are an ingredient in cuisines of nearly every continent around the world. Of the several varieties available, the most common are pale tan in color. Black, red, and brown sesame seeds are also sold in some markets. Because sesame seeds have a high oil content, they are best stored in an airtight container in the refrigerator.

POLENTA MUFFINS WITH FRESH HERBS

Preheat the oven to 375°F (190°C). Grease 14 standard muffin cups with butter or butter-flavored nonstick cooking spray; fill the unused cups one-third full with water to prevent warping.

In a bowl, stir together the all-purpose flour, polenta, cake flour, sugar, baking powder, baking soda, and salt. Using an electric mixer on low speed, add the butter and olive oil and beat until thick crumbs form. Add the eggs, buttermilk, parsley, chives, and savory. Beat just until the mixture is smooth and the herbs are evenly distributed. Do not overbeat.

Spoon the batter into each muffin cup, filling it level with the rim of the cup.

Bake until golden, dry, and springy to the touch, 20–25 minutes. A toothpick inserted into the center of a muffin should come out clean. Transfer the pan(s) to a wire rack and let cool for 5 minutes. Unmold the muffins. Serve them warm or at room temperature, with butter.

MAKES 14 MUFFINS

POLENTA

These muffins are inspired by Italian polenta, a term that refers to cornmeal that is cooked in water or stock and eaten while soft for breakfast or as a side dish. The traditional preparation uses coarse-ground cornmeal. For these muffins, medium-ground cornmeal may be substituted for Italian polenta and will result in muffins with a slightly different, but equally appealing texture. Instant polenta is also available but lacks the hearty texture of the long-cooking variety.

1½ cups (7½ oz/235 g) all-purpose (plain) flour

1¼ cups (6½ oz/200 g) regular or instant polenta

¾ cup (3 oz/90 g) cake (soft-wheat) flour

¼ cup (2 oz/60 g) sugar

1 tablespoon baking powder

1 teaspoon baking soda (bicarbonate of soda)

1½ teaspoons salt

½ cup (4 oz/125 g) cold unsalted butter, cut into small pieces

⅓ cup (3 fl oz/80 ml) olive oil

3 large eggs

1⅓ cups (11 fl oz/345 ml) buttermilk

¼ cup (½ oz/15 g) packed chopped fresh flat-leaf (Italian) parsley

2 tablespoons minced fresh chives

2 tablespoons minced fresh savory, marjoram, or basil

BACON AND GRUYÈRE MUFFINS

7 or 8 thin slices smoked bacon

2 cups (10 oz/315 g) all-purpose (plain) flour

2 tablespoons sugar

1 tablespoon baking powder

½ teaspoon salt

1 large egg

4 tablespoons (2 oz/60 g) unsalted butter, melted (see Notes)

1 cup (8 fl oz/250 ml) milk

2 tablespoons sour cream or plain yogurt

¾ cup (3 oz/90 g) finely diced Gruyère or Swiss cheese

Preheat the oven to 400°F (200°C). Grease 9 standard muffin cups with butter or butter-flavored nonstick cooking spray; fill the unused cups one-third full with water to prevent warping.

In a frying pan over medium-high heat, cook the bacon slices until crisp, 6–8 minutes, turning as needed. Using tongs, transfer to paper towels to drain. Let the bacon cool, then crumble. Set aside.

In a bowl, stir together the flour, sugar, baking powder, and salt.

In another bowl, whisk together the egg, melted butter, milk, and sour cream until blended. Add the egg mixture to the dry ingredients and stir just until evenly moistened. The batter will be slightly lumpy. Using a large rubber spatula, fold in the bacon and cheese just until evenly distributed, no more than a few strokes. Do not overmix.

Spoon the batter into each muffin cup, filling it level with the rim of the cup.

Bake until golden, dry, and springy to the touch, 20–25 minutes. A toothpick inserted into the center of a muffin should come out clean. Transfer the pan to a wire rack and let cool for 5 minutes. Unmold the muffins. Serve warm or at room temperature.

Notes: For added bacon flavor, replace 2 tablespoons of the melted butter with 2 tablespoons bacon fat. If not serving the muffins immediately, store them in the refrigerator.

Serving Tip: These muffins make great accompaniments to soups, salads, and omelets.

MAKES 9 MUFFINS

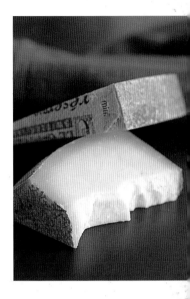

GRUYÈRE CHEESE

This cow's-milk cheese was originally produced exclusively in Switzerland in huge wheels and aged for nearly a year, but is now made outside the country as well. Considered a gastronomic delight, it has a sweet, nutty flavor, is pale yellow in color, and has a firm texture dotted with pea-sized holes. Gruyère is a premier cheese for cooking, as it melts perfectly. Although domestic Swiss cheese may be substituted, it lacks the distinctive flavor of Gruyère.

MUFFINS FLORENTINE

Preheat the oven to 375°F (190°C). Grease 12 standard muffin cups with butter or butter-flavored nonstick cooking spray.

In a bowl, stir together the flour, baking powder, and salt.

In another bowl, whisk together the eggs, olive oil, and milk. Stir in the spinach until well blended. Make a well in the center of the dry ingredients and add the spinach mixture, stirring just until evenly moistened. The batter will be slightly lumpy. Using a large rubber spatula, fold in the pesto and cheese just until evenly distributed. Some streaks of pesto may remain. Do not overmix.

Spoon the batter into each muffin cup, filling it level with the rim of the cup.

Bake until golden, dry, and springy to the touch, 20–25 minutes. A toothpick inserted into the center of a muffin should come out clean. Transfer the pan to a wire rack and let cool for 5 minutes. Unmold the muffins. Serve warm or at room temperature.

MAKES 12 MUFFINS

PESTO
In a food processor or blender, purée 1 or 2 garlic cloves. Add ¼ cup (1¼ oz/37 g) pine nuts, 1 cup (1 oz/30 g) loosely packed fresh basil leaves, and ½ cup (½ oz/15 g) loosely packed fresh flat-leaf (Italian) parsley leaves, and process until finely chopped. With the machine running, slowly pour in about ½ cup (4 fl oz/125 ml) good-quality olive oil and process briefly to make a coarse paste. Add ½ cup (2 oz/60 g) grated Parmesan cheese and pulse just to incorporate. Season with salt, if desired. Makes about 1 cup (8 fl oz/250 ml). Store the leftover pesto in the refrigerator.

3 cups (15 oz/470 g) all-purpose (plain) flour

1 tablespoon baking powder

1¼ teaspoons salt

3 large eggs, beaten

⅔ cup (5 fl oz/160 ml) olive oil

1 cup (8 fl oz/250 ml) milk

1 package (10 oz/315 g) frozen chopped spinach, thawed and squeezed dry

½ cup (4 fl oz/125 ml) pesto *(far left)*

1 cup (4 oz/125 g) shredded mozzarella cheese

COFFEE CAKES

Once you have learned the simple art of muffin baking, you can use the same quick-mixing techniques to create a giant muffin masterpiece: the homemade coffee cake. Tender in crumb and sweet in taste, coffee cakes are consumed with delight along with a steaming cup of coffee or tea. They often have a sweet topping, glaze, or icing that adds a special dimension of flavor.

SPICED APPLE COFFEE CAKE
68

BROWN SUGAR–MACADAMIA NUT COFFEE CAKE
71

FRESH RASPBERRY–SOUR CREAM CRUMB CAKE
72

PEACH STREUSEL COFFEE CAKE
75

STRAWBERRY-RHUBARB BREAKFAST CAKE
76

CHOCOLATE COFFEE CAKE
79

GINGERBREAD WITH MAPLE WHIPPED CREAM
80

ITALIAN ALMOND COFFEE CAKE
83

SPICED APPLE COFFEE CAKE

Preheat the oven to 350°F (180°C). Grease and flour a 9-inch (23-cm) round springform pan or square baking pan or baking dish (see Note).

In a bowl, stir together the flour, baking powder, and salt.

In another bowl, toss the apples with the juice. In a small bowl, stir together the brown sugar, cardamom, and cinnamon. Add to the apples and toss to coat. Set aside.

In another bowl, using an electric mixer on medium speed, cream together the butter, cream cheese, granulated sugar, and vanilla until light and fluffy. Add the eggs, one at a time, beating well after each addition. Add the dry ingredients in 2 or 3 increments and beat well until smooth. Using a large rubber spatula, gently fold in the apples just until evenly distributed, no more than a few strokes. Do not overmix.

Spoon the batter into the prepared pan and spread evenly.

Bake until the top is golden brown, 60–70 minutes. A toothpick inserted into the center of the cake should come out clean. Transfer the pan to a wire rack and let cool for 5 minutes.

Remove the sides of the springform pan, if using, and place the cake on a wire rack set over a piece of waxed paper to catch any drips. While the cake is warm, drizzle with the glaze. Let the cake cool to room temperature. Cut into wedges or squares to serve.

Note: If using a glass baking dish, reduce the oven temperature to 325°F (165°C).

MAKES ONE 9-INCH (23-CM) CAKE

VANILLA GLAZE

As a delicious final touch, a glaze adds a hint of extra flavor and an attractive sheen to a coffee cake. To make the glaze, in a small bowl, whisk together ¾ cup (3 oz/90 g) confectioners' (icing) sugar, sifted; 2 tablespoons condensed skim milk, warmed; and ½ teaspoon vanilla extract (essence) until smooth and pourable. Adjust the consistency of the glaze by adding more milk, a few drops at a time, if necessary.

1¾ cups (9 oz/280 g) all-purpose (plain) flour

1½ teaspoons baking powder

¼ teaspoon salt

3 tart cooking apples, such as Granny Smith or Braeburn, 1 lb (500 g) total weight, peeled, cored, and coarsely chopped

2 tablespoons strained fresh orange juice, lemon juice, or apple juice

⅓ cup (2½ oz/75 g) firmly packed light brown sugar

1½ teaspoons ground cardamom

1 teaspoon ground cinnamon

½ cup (4 oz/125 g) unsalted butter, at room temperature

8 oz (250 g) cream cheese, at room temperature

1½ cups (12 oz/375 g) granulated sugar

1 teaspoon vanilla extract (essence)

2 large eggs

Vanilla Glaze *(far left)*

BROWN SUGAR–MACADAMIA NUT COFFEE CAKE

FOR THE TOPPING:

⅔ cup (4 oz/125 g)
all-purpose (plain) flour

⅓ cup (3 oz/90 g)
granulated sugar

1 teaspoon ground
cinnamon

½ teaspoon ground ginger

6 tablespoons (3 oz/90 g)
cold unsalted butter

1 cup (5 oz/155 g) unsalted
macadamia nuts

1 cup (5 oz/155 g)
all-purpose (plain) flour

½ cup (2 oz/60 g) cake
(soft-wheat) flour

½ cup (4 oz/125 g) *each*
granulated sugar and firmly
packed light brown sugar

1½ teaspoons baking
powder

1 teaspoon baking soda
(bicarbonate of soda)

¼ teaspoon salt

1 cup (8 oz/250 g) sour
cream

2 large eggs

½ cup (4 fl oz/125 ml)
macadamia nut oil

1½ teaspoons vanilla
extract (essence)

Preheat the oven to 350°F (180°C). Grease a 9-inch (23-cm) round springform pan. Line the bottom with a round of parchment (baking) paper and grease the paper.

To make the topping, stir together the flour, sugar, cinnamon, and ginger in a small bowl. Cut the butter into small pieces and add to the bowl. Using a pastry cutter or your fingers, cut or rub in the butter until coarse crumbs form. Set aside.

Coarsely chop the macadamia nuts and set aside.

In a bowl, stir together the all-purpose and cake flours, granulated and brown sugars, baking powder, baking soda, and salt.

In another bowl, whisk together the sour cream, eggs, oil, and vanilla until well blended. Stir the sour cream mixture into the dry ingredients. Using an electric mixer on medium speed or a wire whisk, beat until smooth and creamy, about 1 minute.

Spoon half of the batter into the prepared pan and spread evenly. Sprinkle evenly with half of the topping. Cover evenly with the remaining batter. Sprinkle evenly with the nuts, gently pressing them into the batter, then cover with the remaining topping.

Bake until the topping is golden brown, 40–45 minutes. A toothpick inserted into the center of the cake should come out clean. Transfer the pan to a wire rack and let cool for 20 minutes. Remove the sides of the springform pan. Serve warm or at room temperature, cut into wedges.

Note: Canola oil may be substituted for the macadamia nut oil, if the latter is unavailable.

MAKES ONE 9-INCH (23-CM) CAKE

MACADAMIA NUTS

Buttery-rich macadamia nuts have a pleasurable melt-in-your-mouth consistency. Native to Australia, macadamia trees have been planted in Hawaii, where they flourish. Because the shells are very hard, the nuts are usually sold shelled in vacuum-packed jars or in bulk. Shelled nuts go rancid quickly and therefore should be used immediately or stored in the refrigerator. The delicious oil extracted from macadamias is extremely low in saturated fats, free of cholesterol, and high in omega-3 fatty acids, making it healthier than olive oil. The oil should also be refrigerated.

FRESH RASPBERRY–SOUR CREAM CRUMB CAKE

CRUMB TOPPINGS

Crumbly sweet toppings are sprinkled as a final layer on top of coffee cakes or muffins before baking or are sometimes used as a filling. Another term for this common topping is *streusel,* a German word that means "sprinkle." Such toppings consist of flour; sugar; sometimes spices, nuts, or citrus zest; and butter. The butter, either melted or cut into pieces, is worked into the flour and other ingredients to form coarse crumbs. Streusel toppings bake into a crumbly or crusty texture, depending on the ingredients used.

Preheat the oven to 350°F (180°C). Grease and flour a 10-inch (25-cm) round springform pan.

To make the crumb topping, stir together the flour, sugar, and zest in a small bowl. Add the melted butter and stir with a fork until the mixture is crumbly. Set aside.

To make the cake, in a bowl, stir together the flour, sugar, baking powder, baking soda, and salt.

In another bowl, whisk together the eggs, sour cream, and vanilla until well blended. Make a well in the center of the dry ingredients and add the sour cream mixture. Beat until smooth and fluffy, about 2 minutes.

Spoon the batter into the prepared pan and spread evenly. Cover evenly with the raspberries. Sprinkle the crumb topping evenly over the berries.

Bake until the topping is golden brown, 38–42 minutes. A toothpick inserted into the center of the cake should come out clean. Transfer the pan to a wire rack and let cool for 20 minutes. Remove the sides of the springform pan. Dust with the confectioners' sugar and serve warm or at room temperature, cut into wedges.

MAKES ONE 10-INCH (25-CM) CAKE

FOR THE CRUMB TOPPING:

1 cup (5 oz/155 g) all-purpose (plain) flour

⅔ cup (5 oz/155 g) granulated sugar

Grated zest of 1 lemon

½ cup (4 oz/125 g) unsalted butter, melted

FOR THE CAKE:

1¾ cups (9 oz/280 g) all-purpose (plain) flour

1 cup (8 oz/250 g) granulated sugar

2 teaspoons baking powder

¼ teaspoon baking soda (bicarbonate of soda)

¼ teaspoon salt

3 large eggs

1 cup (8 oz/250 g) sour cream

1 teaspoon vanilla extract (essence)

2 cups (8 oz/250 g) fresh raspberries

2 tablespoons confectioners' (icing) sugar

PEACH STREUSEL COFFEE CAKE

FOR THE STREUSEL:

¾ cup (4 oz/125 g)
all-purpose (plain) flour

⅓ cup (2½ oz/75 g) firmly
packed light brown sugar

¼ cup (2 oz/60 g)
granulated sugar

1 teaspoon ground
cinnamon

6 tablespoons (3 oz/90 g)
cold unsalted butter, cut
into small pieces

FOR THE CAKE:

1½ cups (7½ oz/235 g)
all-purpose (plain) flour

¾ cup (6 oz/185 g)
granulated sugar

2 teaspoons baking powder

½ teaspoon salt

1 large egg

4 tablespoons (2 oz/60 g)
unsalted butter, melted

½ cup (4 fl oz/125 ml) milk

1½ teaspoons vanilla
extract (essence)

1 teaspoon almond extract
(essence)

2 firm, ripe peaches, 1 lb
(500 g) total, peeled *(far
right)*, pitted, and sliced
1 inch (2.5 cm) thick

Preheat the oven to 350°F (180°C). Grease and flour a 9-inch (23-cm) round springform pan or square baking pan or baking dish (see Note).

To make the streusel, stir together the flour, brown and granulated sugars, and cinnamon in a bowl. Using a pastry cutter or your fingers, cut or rub in the butter until coarse crumbs form. Set aside.

To make the cake, in a bowl, stir together the flour, sugar, baking powder, and salt.

In another bowl, using an electric mixer on medium speed or a wire whisk, beat the egg, melted butter, milk, and vanilla and almond extracts until creamy, about 1 minute. Add to the dry ingredients and beat just until evenly moistened. There should be no lumps or dry spots. Do not overmix.

Spoon the batter into the prepared pan and spread evenly. If using a springform pan, arrange the peach slices in concentric circles from the pan sides to the center. If using a square pan, arrange the slices in rows. Gently press the slices into the batter. Sprinkle evenly with the streusel.

Bake until the topping is golden brown, 40–45 minutes. A toothpick inserted into the center of the cake should come out clean. Transfer the pan to a wire rack and let cool for 20 minutes. Remove the sides of the springform pan, if using. Serve warm or at room temperature, cut into wedges or squares.

Note: If using a glass baking dish, reduce the oven temperature to 325°F (165°C).

MAKES ONE 9-INCH (23-CM) CAKE

PEACHES

Any peach variety is delicious in this coffee cake, from fruits that are bright yellow-orange with a rosy blush to those that are the palest white. Even ripe peaches, however, may be difficult to peel. To peel them easily, bring a saucepan three-fourths full of water to a boil. Using a small, sharp knife, cut a shallow X on the blossom end of each peach. Immerse the peaches in the boiling water for 20–30 seconds. Lift out with a slotted spoon and let cool on a work surface. Slip off the skins, using your fingers or the knife.

STRAWBERRY-RHUBARB BREAKFAST CAKE

Preheat the oven to 350°F (180°C). Grease a 9-inch (23-cm) angel food cake pan with a removable bottom.

To make the topping, stir together the sugar and cinnamon in a small bowl. Set aside.

To make the cake, in a large bowl, using an electric mixer on medium-high speed, beat the eggs and sugar for about 1 minute. Add the oil and beat on high speed until thick and pale, about 2 minutes.

In another bowl, stir together the flour, baking soda, baking powder, cinnamon, mace, and salt. Add the egg mixture and, using the mixer on low speed or a wooden spoon, beat until thoroughly blended, about 1 minute. Add the strawberries (and their juice, if any) and the rhubarb and, using a large rubber spatula, gently fold in just until evenly distributed. Take care not to break up the fruit. Do not overmix.

Spoon the batter into the prepared pan and spread evenly. Sprinkle evenly with the topping.

Bake until the topping is golden brown, 60–70 minutes. A tooth-pick inserted into the center of the cake should come out clean. Run a knife between the cake and the sides of the pan, and lift up the center tube to separate the cake from the pan sides. Place on a wire rack to cool completely. Run a knife under the bottom and around the sides of the tube, invert the cake to remove the tube, then place the cake upright on a serving plate.

MAKES ONE 9-INCH (23-CM) TUBE CAKE

RHUBARB

Fresh field-grown rhubarb is sold in long, crisp, red or pale pink stalks in the late spring and early summer. Hot house–grown rhubarb is available year-round in some regions. Before the crop reaches market, the leaves are trimmed from the stalks and discarded since they contain high amounts of toxic oxalic acid. Although tart rhubarb is technically a vegetable, it is cooked and sweetened like a fruit. Combining rhubarb with strawberries is a popular pairing. The flavors are pleasantly contrasting, and the berries help sweeten the rhubarb.

FOR THE TOPPING:

2 tablespoons sugar

½ teaspoon ground cinnamon

FOR THE CAKE:

4 large eggs

1⅓ cups (11 oz/345 g) sugar

¾ cup (6 fl oz/180 ml) canola oil or walnut oil

3 cups (15 oz/470 g) all-purpose (plain) flour

2 teaspoons baking soda (bicarbonate of soda)

1 teaspoon baking powder

2 teaspoons ground cinnamon

1 teaspoon ground mace

1 teaspoon salt

4 cups (1 lb/500 g) fresh strawberries, hulled and coarsely chopped

1 or 2 stalks fresh rhubarb, 4 oz (125 g) total weight, cut crosswise into ½-inch (12-mm) slices, or 1 cup (8 oz/250 g) thawed frozen sliced rhubarb

CHOCOLATE COFFEE CAKE

FOR THE STREUSEL:

⅔ cup (4 oz/125 g)
all-purpose (plain) flour

½ cup (3½ oz/105 g) firmly
packed light brown sugar

½ teaspoon ground
cinnamon

6 tablespoons (3 oz/90 g)
cold unsalted butter

¾ cup (4½ oz/140 g)
chocolate chips (see Notes)

1½ cups (7½ oz/235 g)
all-purpose (plain) flour

½ cup (2 oz/60 g) cake
(soft-wheat) flour

⅔ cup (2 oz/60 g)
unsweetened Dutch-
process cocoa powder

1 teaspoon *each* baking
soda (bicarbonate of soda)
and baking powder

½ teaspoon salt

½ cup (4 oz/125 g)
unsalted butter

1 cup (8 oz/250 g)
granulated sugar

3 large eggs

1¼ cups (10 oz/315 g)
sour cream

1½ teaspoons vanilla
extract (essence)

Preheat the oven to 350°F (180°C). Grease and flour a 9-by-13-inch (23-by-33-cm) baking pan or dish (see Notes).

To make the streusel, stir together the flour, brown sugar, and cinnamon in a small bowl. Cut the butter into small pieces and add to the bowl. Using a pastry cutter or your fingers, cut or rub in the butter until coarse crumbs form. Stir in the chocolate chips until evenly distributed. Set aside.

In a bowl, stir together the all-purpose and cake flours, cocoa, baking soda, baking powder, and salt.

In another bowl, using an electric mixer on medium speed, cream together the butter and sugar until light and fluffy. Add the eggs, one at a time, beating thoroughly after each addition. Add the dry ingredients in 2 or 3 increments, alternating with the sour cream and vanilla. Using the mixer on low speed, beat until smooth and fluffy, about 2 minutes.

Spoon the batter into the prepared pan and spread evenly. Sprinkle evenly with the streusel.

Bake until the topping is golden brown, 40–45 minutes. A tooth-pick inserted into the center of the cake should come out clean. Transfer the pan to a wire rack and let cool completely. Cut into squares to serve.

Notes: If using a glass baking dish, reduce the oven temperature to 325°F (165°C). Semisweet (plain) or bittersweet chocolate chips may be used in this coffee cake recipe. To intensify the chocolate flavor, add 1½ teaspoons chocolate extract (essence) when beating in the sour cream and vanilla.

MAKES ONE 9-BY-13-INCH (23-BY-33-CM) CAKE

COCOA POWDER

Unsweetened cocoa powder is made from chocolate liquor, the base for all chocolate preparations. Once the cocoa butter has been pressed out, what remains of the liquor is ground into a fine powder. Dutch-process cocoa powder is treated with an alkali, which makes it darker in color, less bitter, and richer in flavor than nonalkalized cocoa. Recipes with Dutch cocoa use slightly more baking powder to maintain the proper acid-alkaline balance. Good brands of cocoa include Dröste, Poulain, Baker's, van Houten, Hershey's European-style, and Ghirardelli.

GINGERBREAD WITH MAPLE WHIPPED CREAM

GINGERBREAD

Among the earliest-known baked sweets, gingerbread is most recognizable as a soft, dark, moist cake flavored with dark molasses, ground dried gingerroot, and other spices such as cinnamon. It is related to firm, dry-textured cookies or breads, such as the French *pain d'épices* and the English parkin. For the best gingerbread, use fresh ground ginger that is gently spicy-hot. Keep in mind that spices lose potency after long storage, so before preparing gingerbread, replace any spices that are more than 6 months old.

Preheat the oven to 350°F (180°C). Grease and flour an 8- or 9-inch (20- or 23-cm) square baking pan or dish (see Note).

In a bowl, stir together the flour, baking soda, salt, ginger, cinnamon, allspice, and cloves.

In another bowl, using an electric mixer on medium speed, cream together the butter and brown sugar until fluffy. Add the eggs, one at a time, beating thoroughly after each addition. Beat in the molasses. Add the dry ingredients in 2 increments, alternating with the buttermilk and vanilla. Beat well until fluffy and smooth yet thick.

Spoon the batter into the prepared pan and spread evenly.

Bake until the top is dry to the touch and the cake pulls away from the sides of the pan, 35–40 minutes. A toothpick inserted into the center of the cake should come out clean. Transfer the pan to a wire rack and let cool for 30 minutes.

To make the whipped cream, using an electric mixer on medium-high speed, beat the cream in a deep bowl just until it begins to thicken. Add the maple syrup and continue beating until soft peaks form.

Serve the gingerbread warm or at room temperature, cut into squares and accompanied with the maple whipped cream.

Note: If using a glass baking dish, reduce the oven temperature to 325°F (165°C).

Make-Ahead Tip: The maple whipped cream can be covered and refrigerated for up to 4 hours before serving. The gingerbread can be covered and stored at room temperature for up to 2 days.

MAKES ONE 8- OR 9-INCH (20- OR 23-INCH) SQUARE CAKE

1½ cups (7½ oz/235 g) all-purpose (plain) flour

½ teaspoon baking soda (bicarbonate of soda)

¼ teaspoon salt

4 teaspoons ground ginger

1¼ teaspoons ground cinnamon

¼ teaspoon ground allspice

¼ teaspoon ground cloves

½ cup (4 oz/125 g) unsalted butter, at room temperature

½ cup (3½ oz/105 g) firmly packed light or dark brown sugar

2 large eggs

⅔ cup (4 oz/125 g) light or dark molasses

⅔ cup (5 fl oz/160 ml) buttermilk

1½ teaspoons vanilla extract (essence)

FOR THE MAPLE WHIPPED CREAM:

2 cups (16 fl oz/500 ml) cold heavy (double) cream

⅓ cup (4 fl oz/125 ml) pure maple syrup

ITALIAN ALMOND COFFEE CAKE

FOR THE ALMOND CAKE:

⅔ cup (3 oz/90 g) slivered blanched almonds

3¼ cups (16½ oz/515 g) all-purpose (plain) flour

⅔ cup (5 oz/155 g) firmly packed light brown sugar

Grated zest of 2 lemons

1 tablespoon baking powder

Pinch of salt

¾ cup (6 oz/185 g) plus 2 tablespoons cold unsalted butter

1 large egg

2 teaspoons pure vanilla extract (essence)

FOR THE FILLING:

4 oz (125 g) semisweet (plain) chocolate

3½ cups (15 oz/470 g) whole-milk ricotta cheese

Grated zest of 1 orange

1 tablespoon golden rum

¾ cup (6 oz/185 g) granulated sugar

Almond Brittle *(far right)*

Confectioners' (icing) sugar for dusting (optional)

To make the almond cake, preheat the oven to 325°F (165°C). Spread the almonds on a baking sheet and toast, stirring twice, until light brown, 8–10 minutes. Transfer to a plate and let cool slightly, then pour into a food processor. Add ¼ cup (1½ oz/45 g) of the flour and process until a finely ground nut flour forms.

In a stand mixer fitted with the paddle attachment, combine the remaining 3 cups (15 oz/470 g) flour, nut flour, brown sugar, lemon zest, baking powder, and salt. Cut the butter into small pieces and add to the bowl. On low speed, mix in the butter until fine crumbs form. In a small bowl, whisk together the egg and vanilla until blended, then add to the flour mixture. Mix lightly, just until evenly moistened. The batter should be crumbly.

To make the filling, coarsely chop the chocolate. Combine the ricotta, orange zest, rum, and sugar in a bowl. Using the mixer on medium speed, beat until smooth and fluffy. Fold in the chocolate and almond brittle just until evenly distributed.

Grease a 10-inch (25-cm) round springform pan. Increase the oven temperature to 350°F (180°C). Pour half of the cake batter into the prepared pan and, using a large rubber spatula, mound it slightly higher around the edges than in the center. Gently and evenly tamp down with the spatula to flatten any bubbles (do not press firmly). Spread the cheese filling over the batter in an even layer, leaving a 1-inch (2.5-cm) margin around the edge. Spread the remaining batter in an even layer over the cheese filling right up to the pan sides. Gently and evenly tamp to flatten the batter.

Bake until the top is golden brown, 40–45 minutes. Transfer the pan to a wire rack and let cool completely. Remove the sides of the springform pan. If desired, dust with confectioners' sugar. Serve at room temperature, cut into wedges.

MAKES ONE 10-INCH (25-CM) CAKE

ALMOND BRITTLE

The brittle adds texture to a coffee cake inspired by the Italian *crostata di ricotta*. To make the brittle, grease a baking sheet and a large metal spatula. In a large, heavy frying pan over medium heat, cook ⅓ cup (3 oz/90 g) granulated sugar, shaking gently, until it liquefies and turns golden. Take care not to splash; the sugar will be scalding hot. Remove from the heat and stir in ⅔ cup (3 oz/90 g) slivered blanched almonds. Pour onto the prepared sheet and press with the spatula into a single layer. Let cool to room temperature, then break into ½-inch (12-mm) pieces.

QUICK LOAF
BREADS

Quick loaf breads call for the same techniques used for making muffins, and it is no surprise that both share many flavorful ingredients, such as dried fruits and nuts. Also like muffins, many breads bake up with a slightly domed top. Thick slices of the following quick breads can be enjoyed at breakfast or afternoon tea, with a main meal, or for dessert.

ORANGE-NUT BREAD

Preheat the oven to 325°F (165°C). Grease an 8½-by-4½-inch (21.5-by-11.5-cm) loaf pan or spray with nonstick cooking spray.

In a bowl, stir together the flour, sugar, baking powder, salt, and zest. Add the nuts and stir until evenly distributed. Make a well in the center and add the melted butter, eggs, orange juice, and vanilla. Stir until smooth.

Spoon the batter into the prepared pan.

Bake until the top is browned and firm and the loaf begins to pull away from the sides of the pan, 50–60 minutes. A toothpick inserted into the center of the loaf should come out clean. Transfer the pan to a wire rack and let cool for 10 minutes. Unmold the loaf onto the rack and let cool completely. Serve at room temperature, cut into thick slices.

MAKES ONE 8½-BY-4½-INCH (21.5-BY-11.5-CM) LOAF

2 cups (10 oz/315 g) all-purpose (plain) flour

1 cup (8 oz/250 g) sugar

1 tablespoon baking powder

½ teaspoon salt

Grated zest of 1 orange

¾ cup (3 oz/90 g) walnuts, pecans, hazelnuts, or almonds, coarsely chopped

¼ cup (2 oz/60 g) unsalted butter, melted

2 large eggs, beaten

¾ cup (6 fl oz/180 ml) strained fresh orange juice

1 teaspoon vanilla extract (essence)

ZESTING AND JUICING CITRUS

Citrus juice and zest are popular flavorings in baked goods. When a recipe calls for both, first remove the zest. Scrub the fruit, then pull a zester or a Microplane grater across the rind to yield thin strips of zest while leaving the pith behind. Wider and longer strips may be removed with a paring knife or vegetable peeler, then cut into smaller pieces. Tools for juicing citrus include a handheld wooden reamer, a reamer set into a bowl with a spout, a mechanical citrus press, and an electric reamer. The juice should be strained to remove seeds and pulp.

PUMPKIN BREAD WITH DATES

1½ cups (12 oz/375 g) sugar

1 cup (8 oz/250 g) canned pumpkin purée

2 large eggs

½ cup (4 fl oz/125 ml) nut oil, such as walnut or almond, or sunflower seed oil

1¾ cups (9 oz/280 g) all-purpose (plain) flour

1 teaspoon baking soda (bicarbonate of soda)

½ teaspoon baking powder

½ teaspoon salt

½ teaspoon ground cinnamon

½ teaspoon ground cloves

½ teaspoon freshly grated nutmeg

1 cup (6 oz/185 g) coarsely chopped pitted dates

Preheat the oven to 350°F (180°C). Grease a 9-by-5-inch (23-by-13-cm) loaf pan or spray with nonstick cooking spray.

In a bowl, whisk together the sugar, pumpkin pureé, eggs, and oil until smooth, about 1 minute.

In another bowl, stir together the flour, baking soda, baking powder, salt, cinnamon, cloves, and nutmeg. Add the dry ingredients to the pumpkin mixture and beat until smooth and well combined, 1–2 minutes. The batter will be thick. Using a large rubber spatula, fold in the dates just until evenly distributed, no more than a few strokes. Do not overmix.

Spoon the batter into the prepared pan.

Bake until the top is browned and crusty and develops a long center crack, 60–70 minutes. A toothpick inserted into the center of the loaf should come out clean. Transfer the pan to a wire rack and let cool for 10 minutes. Unmold the loaf onto the rack and let cool completely. Serve at room temperature, cut into thick slices.

MAKES ONE 9-BY-5-INCH (23-BY-13-CM) LOAF

DATES
The handsome date palm flourishes in the desert climates of the Middle East and North Africa and in Southern California. The buttery rich fruits grow in large bunches containing up to a thousand dates. Varying from oval to elongated, they have a paper-thin skin and a long pit. Dates are classified as soft, semidry, or dry, according to their moisture content. Medjool, Khadrawy, and Halawy are the commonly marketed soft dates. Deglet Noor and Zahidy are the most popular semidry dates. Whole and pitted dates are available year-round.

OATMEAL-RAISIN BREAD

Preheat the oven to 350°F (180°C). Grease a 9-by-5-inch (23-by-13-cm) loaf pan or spray with nonstick cooking spray.

In a bowl, stir together the flour, oats, raisins, ¾ cup (6 oz/185 g) brown sugar, baking powder, baking soda, salt, cinnamon, nutmeg, and allspice. Make a well in the center and add the eggs, oil, applesauce, and buttermilk. Stir just until evenly moistened, 15–20 strokes. The batter will be slightly lumpy. Do not overmix.

Spoon the batter into the prepared pan. If desired, sprinkle evenly with the 1–2 tablespoons brown sugar.

Bake until the top is well browned and firm and the loaf begins to pull away from the sides of the pan, 40–50 minutes. A toothpick inserted into the center of the loaf should come out clean. Transfer the pan to a wire rack and let cool for 10 minutes. Unmold the loaf onto the rack. Serve at room temperature, cut into thick slices. Alternatively, wrap tightly in plastic wrap and refrigerate for at least 8 hours, or up to 4 days. The loaf slices best when cold.

Note: When measuring the applesauce for this recipe, use a cup for measuring liquids, such as a glass measuring pitcher.

MAKES ONE 9-BY-5-INCH (23-BY-13-CM) LOAF

GOLDEN RAISINS

As the most common dried fruit used in baking, raisins provide intense bursts of flavor. Dark raisins are made by sun-drying grapes, most commonly seedless Thompson grapes. Golden raisins, also known as sultanas, are made with the same grapes as dark raisins, but instead of sun-dried, the grapes are bleached with sulphur dioxide and then mechanically dried in a dehydrator, which produces a plump result. Store both raisin types in covered containers at room temperature for up to a month or in the refrigerator for up to 6 months.

1¼ cups (6½ oz/200 g) all-purpose (plain) flour

1 cup (3½ oz/105 g) quick-cooking rolled oats

⅔ cup (4 oz/125 g) golden raisins (sultanas), or a mixture of golden raisins and dried cherries

¾ cup (6 oz/185 g) firmly packed light brown sugar

1½ teaspoons baking powder

1 teaspoon baking soda (bicarbonate of soda)

½ teaspoon salt

1½ teaspoons ground cinnamon

½ teaspoon freshly grated nutmeg

¼ teaspoon ground allspice

2 large eggs, beaten

⅓ cup (3 fl oz/80 ml) almond oil or canola oil

¾ cup (7 oz/220 g) unsweetened applesauce (page 29; see Note)

½ cup (4 fl oz/125 ml) buttermilk

1–2 tablespoons firmly packed light brown sugar (optional)

CORN BREAD WITH CORN KERNELS

¾ cup (6 oz/185 g) unsalted butter, at room temperature

1¼ cups (10 oz/315 g) sugar

3 large eggs

1½ cups (7½ oz/235 g) fine- to medium-grind yellow cornmeal, preferably stone-ground

1 cup (4 oz/125 g) cake (soft-wheat) flour

½ cup (2½ oz/75 g) all-purpose (plain) flour

⅓ cup (2 oz/60 g) whole-wheat (wholemeal) pastry flour or corn flour (see Notes)

1 tablespoon baking powder

1 teaspoon salt

2 cups (16 fl oz/500 ml) buttermilk

1½ cups (9 oz/280 g) fresh or thawed frozen corn kernels, or 1 can (8¾ oz/270 g) whole-kernel corn, drained

Preheat the oven to 400°F (200°C). Grease a 10-inch (25-cm) round springform pan or 9-by-13-inch (23-by-33-cm) glass baking dish (see Notes) or spray with nonstick cooking spray.

In a bowl, using an electric mixer on medium speed, cream together the butter and sugar until light and fluffy. Add the eggs, one at a time, beating well after each addition.

In another bowl, stir together the cornmeal; the cake, all-purpose, and whole-wheat pastry flours; the baking powder; and the salt. Using the mixer on low speed, add to the creamed mixture in 2 increments, alternating with the buttermilk. Beat until smooth and well combined. Using a large rubber spatula, fold in the corn kernels just until evenly distributed, no more than a few strokes. Do not overmix.

Pour the batter into the prepared pan.

Bake until the bread is golden brown around the edges and begins to pull away from the sides of the pan, 35–40 minutes. A toothpick inserted into the center of the bread should come out clean. Transfer the pan to a wire rack and let cool for 15 minutes. Remove the sides of the springform pan, if using. Serve warm or at room temperature, cut into wedges or squares.

Notes: If using a glass baking dish, reduce the oven temperature to 375°F (190°C). This bread is best served the day it is made. If there are leftovers, store, wrapped in plastic, in the refrigerator. Look for whole-wheat pastry flour and corn flour in natural-foods stores.

MAKES ONE 10-INCH (25-CM) ROUND OR 9-BY-13-INCH (23-BY-33-CM) RECTANGULAR BREAD

FOLDING

Using this technique allows the cook to combine two mixtures or ingredients with markedly different densities. Begin by putting the ingredient or mixture to be incorporated (in this recipe, corn kernels) on top of the batter. Using a large rubber spatula, gently cut down through the center of the batter to the bottom of the bowl and pull the spatula in a circular motion up and over the contents, thereby folding in the corn without overhandling the batter. Rotate the bowl a quarter turn and repeat the motion. Continue just until the ingredient is evenly distributed.

PRUNE BREAD

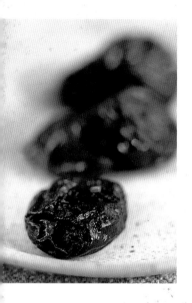

Preheat the oven to 350°F (180°C). Grease a 9-by-5-inch (23-by-13-cm) loaf pan or spray with nonstick cooking spray.

Put the prunes in a bowl and add the boiling water and vanilla. Let stand at room temperature until cool, 30–60 minutes.

In a bowl, stir together the flour, sugar, walnuts, baking powder, baking soda, salt, cinnamon, and nutmeg. Make a well in the center and add the egg, melted butter, and prune mixture with its liquid. Stir just until evenly moistened.

Spoon the batter into the prepared pan.

Bake until the top is browned and firm and the loaf begins to pull away from the sides of the pan, 55–60 minutes. A toothpick inserted into the center of the loaf should come out clean. Transfer the pan to a wire rack and let cool for 10 minutes. Unmold the loaf onto the rack and let cool completely. Wrap the loaf tightly in plastic wrap and store at room temperature overnight. Cut into thick slices and serve.

MAKES ONE 9-BY-5-INCH (23-BY-13-CM) LOAF

PRUNES

Plums, a stone fruit like peaches, are dried to produce prunes, resulting in dried fruits with a dark, firm flesh and a high sugar content. Prunes are categorized by size, ranging from small to jumbo, with the larger grades having an appealing plumpness. Most of the prunes sold in the United States are produced in California. One of the common plums used is the d'Agen from France. For this recipe, look for prunes sold in airtight packages that help preserve their moisture content. Store at room temperature for up to a month or in the refrigerator for up to 6 months.

12 oz (375 g) moist-pack pitted prunes, coarsely chopped

1 cup (8 fl oz/250 ml) boiling water

1 teaspoon vanilla extract (essence)

2 cups (10 oz/315 g) all-purpose (plain) flour

¾ cup (6 oz/185 g) sugar

¾ cup (3 oz/90 g) walnuts, chopped

2 teaspoons baking powder

1 teaspoon baking soda (bicarbonate of soda)

½ teaspoon salt

1 teaspoon ground cinnamon

½ teaspoon freshly grated nutmeg

1 large egg, beaten

4 tablespoons (2 oz/60 g) unsalted butter, melted

APRICOT BREAD WITH HAZELNUTS

22 dried apricot halves, coarsely chopped

½ cup (3 oz/90 g) dried currants

1 cup (8 fl oz/250 ml) boiling water

3 cups (15 oz/470 g) all-purpose (plain) flour

1 cup (7 oz/220 g) firmly packed light brown sugar

1 tablespoon baking powder

½ teaspoon baking soda (bicarbonate of soda)

1 teaspoon salt

3 tablespoons unsalted butter, melted, or hazelnut oil

2 large eggs, beaten

1⅓ cups (11 fl oz/345 ml) buttermilk

1 cup (4 oz/125 g) hazelnuts, chopped

Put the apricots and currants in a bowl. Add the boiling water. Set aside at room temperature and let cool to lukewarm, about 1 hour.

Preheat the oven to 350°F (180°C). Grease and flour four 6-by-3½-inch (15-by-9-cm) loaf pans or spray with nonstick cooking spray.

In a bowl, stir together the flour, brown sugar, baking powder, baking soda, and salt. Make a well in the center and add the melted butter, eggs, and buttermilk. Beat until smooth, about 1 minute. Add the apricots and currants with their liquid and the hazelnuts. Beat just until blended and the fruit and nuts are evenly distributed. Do not overmix.

Spoon the batter into the prepared pans.

Bake until the tops are browned and firm and the loaves begin to pull away from the sides of the pans, 45–50 minutes. A toothpick inserted into the center of a loaf should come out clean. Immediately unmold the loaves onto wire racks and let cool completely. Wrap the loaves tightly in plastic wrap and refrigerate for at least 8 hours, or up to 4 days. Cut into thick slices and serve.

MAKES FOUR 6-BY-3½-INCH (15-BY-9-CM) LOAVES

HAZELNUTS

Popular in French and Italian baking, and also known as filberts, these round nuts encased in a hard shell have a delightful crunch and rich, buttery flavor that shine in quick loaf breads, especially in combination with dried fruits. Hazelnuts have a thin inner skin that can be removed, if desired. Bake the nuts on a baking sheet in a preheated 325°F (165°C) oven, stirring occasionally, for about 10 minutes. While the nuts are still warm, wrap in a coarse-textured kitchen towel and rub vigorously to remove most of the skins.

MAPLE-PECAN BREAD

Preheat the oven to 350°F (180°C). Grease a 9-by-5-inch (23-by-13-cm) loaf pan or spray with nonstick cooking spray.

In a food processor, combine half of the pecans and ¾ cup (4 oz/125 g) of the flour. Process until a finely ground nut flour forms. Coarsely chop the remaining pecans and set aside.

In a bowl, stir together the remaining 1¾ cups (9 oz/280 g) flour, nut flour, sugar, baking powder, and salt. Make a well in the center and add the eggs, melted butter, buttermilk, and maple syrup. Stir just until evenly moistened, 15–20 strokes. The batter will be slightly lumpy. Do not overmix. Using a large rubber spatula, fold in the chopped pecans just until evenly distributed, no more than a few strokes. Do not overmix.

Spoon the batter into the prepared pan.

Bake for 30 minutes, then rotate the pan and bake until the top is golden brown, about 30 minutes longer. Reduce the oven temperature to 325°F (165°C) and continue baking until the top is browned and firm and the loaf begins to pull away from the sides of the pan, 10–15 minutes longer. A toothpick inserted into the center of the loaf should come out clean. Transfer the pan to a wire rack and let cool for 10 minutes. Carefully unmold the loaf onto the rack and let cool completely. Wrap tightly in plastic wrap and store at room temperature overnight. Cut into thick slices and serve.

MAKES ONE 9-BY-5-INCH (23-BY-13-CM) LOAF

MAPLE SYRUP

Luxurious, pure maple syrup is a sumptuous taste treat. Once initiated to its special qualities, you will never consider using imitation-flavored sugar syrups. Maple syrup, produced by boiling the sap of the sugar maple tree, is characterized by grade. Grade A Light or Fancy is pale and delicate. Grade A Medium and Dark and Grade B syrups, both excellent for baking, are progressively a bit thicker, darker in color, and slightly stronger in flavor. Grade B syrup, robust in flavor, is the choice of discriminating bakers for its pronounced maple flavor.

1½ cups (6 oz/185 g) pecans

2½ cups (13 oz/405 g) all-purpose (plain) flour

1 cup (8 oz/250 g) sugar

1 tablespoon baking powder

½ teaspoon salt

3 large eggs, beaten

4 tablespoons (2 oz/60 g) unsalted butter, melted

1 cup (8 fl oz/250 ml) buttermilk

¾ cup (9 fl oz/265 ml) pure maple syrup

MUFFIN BASICS

Muffins and quick loaf breads can be savory or sweet; coffee cakes, crowned with a topping, usually star at the breakfast table. All of these breads rely on chemical leaveners, rather than yeast, and are prepared with the same basic ingredients and techniques.

INGREDIENTS

The quality of the ingredients contributes significantly to the taste and texture of finished breads. Flour, leavening, butter or oil, and dairy products, key ingredients in muffins and other quick breads, should be purchased from a reliable source and stored properly to maintain freshness.

FLOURS AND GRAINS

Most of the recipes in this book use all-purpose (plain) flour, sometimes in combination with other flours. All-purpose flour is a mixture of both soft and hard wheats and is ground from the endosperm of the wheat kernel. Unbleached flour, which can be substituted, has not been chemically treated and is not as white as all-purpose, but is regarded as having a better flavor. Several recipes call for cake flour, also called soft-wheat flour. This bleached flour milled from soft wheat is higher in starch and lower in protein than all-purpose flour. It gives coffee cakes, muffins, and quick loaf breads a light, tender crumb.

Using whole-wheat flour adds not only nutrition but also a sweet nutty flavor to breads. The extra boost results from milling whole grains of wheat that still contain the bran and germ. Whole-wheat pastry flour gives breads a tender texture and lightens what would otherwise be a heavy whole-grain batter. Graham flour is a type of coarse whole-wheat flour ground from hard wheat.

Cornmeal, made from yellow, white, or blue corn, is ground fine, medium, or coarse. Whichever color or grind you prefer, seek out stone-ground cornmeal for its exceptional flavor. This variety is processed from the whole kernel rather than just the starchy interior endosperm. Corn flour is white or yellow cornmeal that has been ground to a fine texture.

Most flours keep well for up to 6 months in an airtight container stored in a cool, dry place away from light. Whole-wheat flour and stone-ground cornmeal turn rancid quickly and should be placed in containers and refrigerated.

LEAVENERS

Muffins, coffee cakes, and quick loaf breads use a chemical leavener, such as baking powder or baking soda, and sometimes both, plus the actions of creaming and beating in air, to lighten their batters.

Baking soda, also known as bicarbonate of soda, is used when a batter includes buttermilk, yogurt, sour cream, molasses, honey, maple syrup, citrus, or other fresh fruit or fruit juice. Upon contact with these acidic ingredients, baking soda fosters a simple chemical reaction that produces carbon dioxide gas. The carbon dioxide bubbles expand when they come in contact with liquid and continue to expand in the heat of the oven. During baking, the trapped bubbles create steam, which releases into the batter and makes a nicely rounded, moist bread.

A batter using baking soda must be baked shortly after mixing for best results. If it sits long after mixing, it will lose volume.

Baking powder contains both alkaline and acid components. Because it is complete within itself, the batter in which it is used does not have to include an acidic liquid such as buttermilk. Most powders are "double acting," meaning that they react twice: by producing carbon dioxide bubbles in the batter when the dry ingredients are moistened with liquid and again in the heat of the oven. Some bakers prefer non-aluminum baking powder, as it has a less bitter aftertaste.

Batters made with baking powder improve slightly in texture and flavor if allowed to rise at room temperature for 15 to 20 minutes. They may also sit in the refrigerator for up to 24 hours before baking.

Some heavy batters include both types of leaveners, which help them bake into light-textured breads.

Store both types of leaveners in a cool, dry place. They can lose potency over time and should be replaced after 4 to 6 months.

BUTTER AND OIL

Muffins, coffee cakes, and quick loaf breads always call for some type of fat to create appealing texture and contribute to the overall flavor. This may be an oil such as canola or walnut, or a solid fat like butter. Unsalted butter lends a delicate taste to breads and has a lower moisture content than salted butter. If substituting salted butter, cut down on the salt called for in the recipe by half.

Nut oils, which turn rancid easily when exposed to light and heat, should be purchased from a store with a high turnover. Taste an oil after you bring it home, to be sure it is fresh. Nut oils should be refrigerated, then brought to room temperature before using in a recipe.

Each type of fat contributes its own textural qualities. When room-temperature butter is beaten with sugar, the mixture tends to emulsify and expand into a fluffy and creamy consistency, and the fat is uniformly dispersed throughout. By contrast, a sugar-oil mixture will look clumpy and not reach as fluffy a consistency. This batter yields a coarser grain appropriate for muffins.

DAIRY PRODUCTS

Milk, buttermilk, sour cream, and yogurt add wonderful flavor and tenderness to quick breads. When a recipe calls for milk, use regular, low fat, or skim. Fresh buttermilk, a cultured milk product, contributes a silky texture to quick breads. Dried milk powder or dried buttermilk powder are acceptable substitutes for fresh milks.

The best sour cream to use is a brand without additives or preservatives; avoid fat-free types, since the fat in sour cream is essential to a recipe.

Sour cream substitutes work well. Always use plain yogurt, whether whole milk or low fat.

TECHNIQUES

Two basic techniques are used to combine wet and dry ingredients: the muffin method and the creaming method. Each has a defined progression, with slight variations from recipe to recipe.

In the fast-and-easy muffin method, dry and wet ingredients are mixed separately before being combined, as for Country Applesauce Muffins (page 29) and Maple-Pecan Bread (page 98). The basic steps are shown opposite:

1 Mixing dry ingredients: Stir together the flour, leavening, and other dry ingredients so that the leavening is evenly distributed.

2 Combining wet and dry ingredients: Whisk together the wet ingredients until smooth and blended, then add to the dry ingredients. Mix quickly to activate the gluten in the flour only slightly, until the dry ingredients are evenly moistened. The batter may be lumpy; any lumps will vanish during baking. Finally, gently stir or fold in fruits, nuts, or other additions (page 93).

3 Filling the pans: Spoon the batter into greased muffin cups, filling them three-fourths full or even with the rim of the cup.

4 Adding a topping: If the recipe calls for a topping, sprinkle it over the batter, dividing it evenly among the muffins.

Sometimes a well is made in the center of the dry ingredients, and all of the wet ingredients are added to the well. The mixture is then beaten until smooth. In other recipes, the dry ingredients are added to the wet ingredients.

Whatever the instruction, it is important not to overmix a batter, or the finished bread will be tough and often crumbly, with large irregular patterns of holes.

The creaming method takes more time, yet significantly lessens the possibility of overmixing, and the batter bakes up into a finer, moister texture. This method is used for batters with a higher proportion of fat and sugar than those mixed with the muffin method, such as Lemon–Poppy Seed Muffins (page 17), Chocolate Coffee Cake (page 79), and Corn Bread with Corn Kernels (page 93).

Room-temperature fat, usually butter, and sugar are beaten with an electric mixer until light and fluffy. The eggs are added, one at a time, and beaten until thoroughly incorporated, as for a cake batter. The dry ingredients are combined separately and stirred to distribute the leavening. They are added in increments to the egg mixture alternating with any liquid and flavorings, and the batter is beaten just until smooth.

EQUIPMENT

A small, versatile selection of equipment is used for making muffins, coffee cakes, and quick loaf breads.

Indispensable tools for mixing include wooden spoons and large metal whisks. Flat and curved rubber spatulas in large and small sizes should also be kept on hand. Large spatulas are for scraping bowls (always check to make sure ingredients at the very bottom of the bowl have been incorporated into the batter) and for efficiently folding embellishments such as fruits and nuts into batters. Small spatulas are handy for cleaning the beaters of an electric mixer and for smoothing the surface of batters after pouring into a pan. A spring-lever ice-cream scoop is useful for filling muffin cups; a dry measuring cup or a large spoon also works well for this purpose.

Keep toothpicks on hand for testing the interior of a muffin or other quick bread. A long metal or bamboo skewer or a sharp thin-bladed knife also works well for this purpose, as does a cake tester, a piece of stainless steel wire with a heatproof, plastic-coated loop handle. Wire racks are essential for cooling breads in their pans and after unmolding. A small metal spatula is good for coaxing baked muffins from pans.

For slicing quick loaf breads and coffee cakes, be sure to use a serrated knife, which will cut through the breads without compressing them or causing them to crumble.

BAKING PANS

Using the correct pan size is essential. An overfull pan will cause batter to drip over the sides during baking; an underfilled pan will result in unattractive flat-topped muffins and breads. Each recipe is specific about the pan required and the amount of batter to be placed in it, depending on the viscosity of the batter and how much it will expand during baking.

A standard muffin pan contains 12 cups. Each is 2¾ to 3 inches (7 to 7.5 cm) wide by 1¾ inch (4.5 cm) deep, and has a capacity of about ½ cup (4 fl oz/125 ml). Some muffin pans have 6 cups. Restaurant supply stores carry professional muffin tins with 24 standard cups, suitable for large home ovens and recipes with high yields. Muffin pans can also be used for making cupcakes, rolls, and individual custards.

A jumbo, or oversized, muffin pan has 6 cups, each 4 inches (10 cm) wide and 2 inches (5 cm) deep, with a capacity of 1 cup (8 fl oz/250 ml). Muffins baked in this pan are two to three times larger than standard muffins. A miniature muffin pan has 12 or 24 cups, each 2 inches (5 cm) wide by ¾ inch (2 cm) deep, with a capacity of 2 tablespoons.

Recipes for standard muffins can easily be adapted for baking in jumbo or miniature muffin cups. The only element that needs to be adjusted is the baking time: bake jumbo muffins for 8 to 12 minutes longer than specified in a recipe; bake miniature muffins for 5 to 7 minutes less.

Among the other options for muffin recipes, the batter may be baked in a madeleine pan measuring 14 by 7 inches (35 by 18 cm). Each of the pan's twelve shells, measuring about 3 inches (7 cm) long and 2 inches (5 cm) wide, holds the same amount of batter as a miniature muffin cup. Baking time is 15 minutes. Some cooks nowadays like to bake muffin batter in the rings used to make crumpets, which yield muffins that are flat and round, easy to fit into a toaster. The rings, each about 4 inches (10 cm) in diameter and 1 inch (2.5 cm) tall, are set on a baking sheet lined with parchment (baking) paper. About ¼ cup (2 fl oz/ 60 ml) batter is poured into each ring. Thick muffin batters such as Blueberry Muffins (page 10) and Polenta Muffins (page 60) work best; the baking time remains the same.

Standard pans for quick loaf breads measure 9 by 5 inches (23 by 13 cm) and 8½ by 4½ inches (21.5 by 11.5 cm). A standard quick bread loaf can also be made in small loaf pans. A common size is 6 by 3½ inches (15 by 9 cm); other sizes are available in cookware stores. A batter for a 9-by-5-inch pan may be divided between two 6-by-3½-inch pans; the oven temperature should be reduced by one-third.

For most coffee cakes, the same amount of batter will fill a 9- or 10-inch (23- or 25-cm) round spring-form pan or a glass or metal 8- or 9-inch (21- or 23-cm) square cake pan.

Muffin pans, loaf pans, and other baking pans are available with a variety of nonstick finishes, which allow the baked breads to be unmolded without resistance and the pans to be cleaned easily. The oven temperature should be reduced by 25°F (15°C) when using these dark-finish pans— or when using glass pans—in order to avoid overbrowning.

PREPARING PANS

Baking pans need to be greased on the sides and bottoms with butter or oil. The best oil is the one called for in the recipe or a mild oil that will not clash with the other flavors. Butter-flavored nonstick cooking spray is indispensable for evenly greasing muffin cups and other baking pans. Lightly greasing even nonstick pans guarantees that breads can be effortlessly unmolded.

Some recipes call for both greasing and flouring a pan before the batter is added. After coating the pan lightly with oil or butter, add a spoonful of flour, then shake and tilt the pan to distribute the flour evenly. Tap out any excess flour. For especially dense batters, pans are greased and then lined with parchment (baking) paper, which is also lightly greased.

Paper liners for muffin cups are best to use when the muffins will be served at room temperature. The liners will help keep the muffins fresh and will be easier to remove than if the muffins were warm. Liners are not available for jumbo pans, but those used for making candy will fit miniature muffin cups.

If a recipe makes fewer muffins than the number of cups in the pan, fill the empty cups one-third full with water; this prevents the pan from buckling in the oven.

BAKING AND COOLING

The proper baking times are given for each recipe but may need to be adjusted for your particular oven. Use an oven thermometer to check your oven and adjust the temperature as necessary.

The muffins, coffee cakes, and quick loaf breads in this book should be baked on the middle rack of the oven. If using more than one pan, for instance, several small loaf pans, allow at least 2 inches (5 cm) between each pan so heat can circulate. If you are doubling a muffin recipe and using two pans, arrange them side by side rather than on separate racks. Avoid opening the oven until near the end of baking, or it will not maintain the correct heat level, causing the muffins or other quick breads to rise unevenly.

Always test breads 5–10 minutes before the end of the prescribed baking time to make sure that the tops are not browning too fast.

Muffins are done when golden brown around the edges and springy to the touch on top. Most quick loaf breads will have browned tops, and the loaves will be firm, begin to pull away from the pan sides, and have a characteristic crack down the center. Coffee cakes are generally done when the top or topping is golden brown. The interior of a muffin or quick loaf bread should be checked for doneness. When inserted in the center of a muffin or loaf, a toothpick or other tool should come out clean.

Most muffins and quick loaf breads should be cooled in their pans on a wire rack for 5 minutes or more; this allows the heat to dissipate and helps set the tender texture. Then they are turned out of the pans and are placed on the rack to continue cooling. If allowed to cool completely in their pans, the breads can be difficult to unmold, and the bottoms can easily turn soggy.

Many loaves and coffee cakes are easiest to slice when cooled to room temperature, which allows their flavors to meld and their textures to set properly. If sliced too soon after baking, they will be too crumbly. For this reason, some quick loaf breads are wrapped in plastic and refrigerated before serving, or are allowed to stand overnight at room temperature.

STORING

The muffins, coffee cakes, and quick loaf breads in this book store well after they are baked and completely cooled. Muffins can be kept in plastic bags for up to 1 week at room temperature. Muffins containing cheese or other dairy products that can spoil easily should be placed in bags and refrigerated. Most coffee cakes and quick loaf breads store well covered with plastic wrap for 4 days in the refrigerator.

Muffins keep for up to 3 months when frozen in a double layer of zippered freezer bags or in plastic wrap and then aluminum foil before slipping into bags. Some bakers wrap each muffin separately in plastic wrap, so single muffins can easily be removed from the freezer. Quick loaf breads and coffee cakes can be enclosed in freezer bags, or wrapped in plastic wrap and foil beforehand, and stored for up to 2 months. Slices of bread and wedges of coffee cake can be wrapped separately and stored as for individual muffins. Be sure to label and date packages.

To defrost frozen muffins, set them out at room temperature in their wrapping for 20 to 30 minutes. Slightly unwrap quick loaf breads and coffee cakes and allow them to stand for a few hours or overnight.

To reheat quick bread loaves and coffee cakes, unwrap them completely and place on a baking sheet in a preheated 300°F (150°C) oven until heated through, 10–20 minutes. Muffins, slices of quick loaf breads, and wedges of coffee cake need only 5–8 minutes. A microwave works well for reheating individual muffins and servings of a quick loaf bread or coffee cake. Heat for 1 minute, then check at 10-second intervals until warmed to your liking.

ACCOMPANIMENTS

The following recipes will enhance many of the muffin and quick loaf bread recipes throughout this book.

LEMON CURD

Grated zest of 2 large lemons

½ cup (4 fl oz/125 ml) strained fresh lemon juice

3 large eggs

½ cup (4 oz/125 g) sugar

6 tablespoons (3 oz/90 g) unsalted butter, melted

Combine the lemon zest and juice, eggs, and sugar in a blender or food processor and process for 20 seconds. With the machine running, drizzle in the melted butter. Pour into a small saucepan and bring to a low boil over medium heat. Immediately reduce the heat to medium-low and cook, stirring constantly, until the mixture is thick and coats the back of a spoon, about 5 minutes. Transfer to a small bowl and let cool to room temperature. Cover and store in the refrigerator for up to 2 weeks. Bring to room temperature before serving. Makes 1⅓ cups (11 fl oz/340 ml).

PLUM AND HONEY BUTTER

2 lb (1 kg) very ripe plums, pitted and cut into chunks

3 tablespoons thawed frozen orange juice concentrate

3 tablespoons honey

2–3 tablespoons sugar

½ teaspoon ground cinnamon

Preheat the oven to 300°F (150°C). Place the plums, orange juice, honey, sugar to taste, and cinnamon in a food processor. Pulse until the mixture forms a smooth to slightly chunky purée as desired.

Transfer the purée to a 9-by-13-inch (23-by-33-cm) baking dish. Bake uncovered, stirring occasionally to ensure even cooking, until the fruit is reduced by half to a thick purée, about 1¼ hours.

Remove from the oven and let stand until cool. Using a rubber spatula, transfer the butter to a glass jar. Store in the refrigerator for up to 2 weeks. Makes about 2 cups (16 fl oz/500 ml).

Variation Tip: Substitute 2 lb (1 kg) ripe apricots, pitted and cut into chunks, for the plums; use ¼ cup (2 fl oz/60 ml) thawed frozen orange juice concentrate and ¼ cup (3 oz/90 g) honey, and prepare and bake as directed.

MAPLE BUTTER

½ cup (4 oz/125 g) unsalted butter, at room temperature

3 tablespoons pure maple syrup

Cream together the butter and maple syrup in a small bowl until well combined. Store, covered, in the refrigerator for up to 3 days. Bring to room temperature before serving. Makes about ½ cup (4 oz/125 g).

GOAT CHEESE SPREAD

8 oz (250 g) fresh goat cheese, at room temperature

6 oz (185 g) cream cheese, at room temperature

¼ cup (2 oz/60 g) unsalted butter, at room temperature

In a bowl, combine the goat cheese, cream cheese, and butter. Using a wooden spoon or an electric mixer on medium speed, beat together until smooth. Alternatively, combine in a food processor and pulse until smooth.

Using a rubber spatula, transfer into a crock or other container. Cover and store in the refrigerator for up to 1 week. Bring to room temperature before serving. Makes about 2 cups (1 lb/500 g).

Serving Tip: The spread is delicious on both savory and sweet muffins and also on quick loaf breads.

INDEX

SIMON & SCHUSTER SOURCE
A Division of Simon & Schuster, Inc.
1230 Avenue of the Americas
New York, NY 10020

WILLIAMS-SONOMA
Founder and Vice-Chairman: Chuck Williams

WELDON OWEN INC.
Chief Executive Officer: John Owen
President: Terry Newell
Chief Operating Officer: Larry Partington
Vice President, International Sales: Stuart Laurence
Creative Director: Gaye Allen
Series Editor: Sarah Putman Clegg
Managing Editor: Judith Dunham
Editor: Heather Belt
Designer: Teri Gardiner
Production: Chris Hemesath and Teri Bell
Production Assistant: Libby Temple

Weldon Owen wishes to thank the following
people for their generous assistance and support in
producing this book: Copy Editor Carolyn Miller;
Food Stylist Sandra Cook; Assistant Food Stylists
Elisabet der Nederlanden, Ann Tonai, and Melinda
Barsales; Photographer's Assistants Noriko Akiyama
and Heidi Ladendorf; Proofreaders Carrie Bradley and
Linda Bouchard; Production Designer Linda Bouchard;
and Indexer Ken DellaPenta.

Set in Trajan, Utopia, and Vectora.

Williams-Sonoma Collection *Muffins* was
conceived and produced by Weldon Owen Inc.,
814 Montgomery Street, San Francisco,
California 94133, in collaboration with
Williams-Sonoma, 3250 Van Ness Avenue,
San Francisco, California 94109.

A Weldon Owen Production

For information about special discounts for bulk
purchases, please contact Simon & Schuster
Special Sales: 1-800-456-6798 or
business@simonandschuster.com

Color separations by Bright Arts Graphics
Singapore (Pte.) Ltd.
Printed and bound in Singapore by Tien Wah
Press (Pte.) Ltd.

First printed in 2003.

10 9 8 7 6 5 4 3

Library of Congress Cataloging-in-Publication
Data is available.

ISBN 0-7432-5396-5

A NOTE ON WEIGHTS AND MEASURES

All recipes include customary U.S. and metric measurements. Metric conversions are based on
a standard developed for these books and have been rounded off. Actual weights may vary.